T5-CRZ-296

TOWARD A SCIENTIFIC ARCHITECTURE

390150 49181228

TOWARD A SCIENTIFIC ARCHITECTURE

Yona Friedman

translated by Cynthia Lang

The MIT Press
Cambridge, Massachusetts, and London, England

AAEL
Architectural
Library
NA
2500
.F933

Chapters 1-7 were originally published in French under the title *Vers une architecture scientifique* by Editions Pierre Belfond, Paris.

English translation and revision copyright © 1975 by
The Massachusetts Institute of Technology

All rights reserved. No part of this book may be reproduced in any form or by any means, electronic or mechanical, including photocopying, recording, or by any information storage and retrieval system, without permission in writing from the publisher.

This book was set in IBM Composer Univers
by Technical Composition,
printed on R & E Book,
and bound in Columbia Millbank Vellum
by The Colonial Press Inc.
in the United States of America

Library of Congress Cataloging in Publication Data

Friedman, Yona, 1923-
    Toward a scientific architecture.

    Translation of Vers une architecture scientifique.
    1. Architecture. I. Title.
NA2500.F7413   720'.1   75-8769
ISBN 0-262-06058-2

1130879-200

CONTENTS

FOREWORD TO THE ENGLISH-LANGUAGE EDITION by
Nicholas P. Negroponte   ix

PERSPECTIVE   xi

1 DEMOCRATIZATION   1
1.1   The Many   1
1.2   Information Processing: The Information Circuit between User and Planner   4
1.3   The Solution: Direct Feedback from the User   6
1.4   Architecture: A "Teachable" Science   11
1.5   Architecture Can Be Taught at the Primary Level   13

2 ESSENTIALS OF THE METHOD   15
2.1   Objective and Intuitive Systems   15
2.2   A Complete List of Solutions as an Acceptable Answer   18
2.3   Choosing an Appropriate Axiomatics   20
2.4   Axioms to Describe the Work of Architects and Planners   25
2.5   A Mapping for Architects and Planners   26
2.6   Constructing Combinatorial Lists   29

3 THE NEW TASK OF ARCHITECTS AND PLANNERS   33
3.1   Like Eating Out   33
3.2   Building the Repertoire   35
3.3   The Path Matrix   40
3.4   The Supporting Network and Its Hardware Counterpart   43
3.5   A Technological Necessity: The Chance to Make Modifications   47
3.6   Keeping a History of Modifications   49
3.7   An Application of the Repertoire: The Flatwriter   53
Conclusion   60

4 URBAN MECHANISMS   62
4.1   Complete Planar Graphs with $n \geqslant 7$: Crossovers and Potential Conflicts   62
4.2   Networks   64

4.3   Example of an Analysis Using Networks: Patterns of
Transportation   68

4.4   How Do You Observe a City?   72

4.5   The Urban Mechanism   74

4.6   Probability as a Frequency Concept or as a Gauge   76

4.7   The Effort Map: Its Characteristics and Use   78

4.8   A History Depicted by Urban Mechanisms   82

4.9   The Unpredictability of History   86

4.10   Applying the Method of Urban Mechanisms   87

5 GENERAL APPLICATIONS OF THE METHOD   93

5.1   Looking for Laws of Nature in Histories   93

5.2   Constructing the Field of Reference: Types of Human
Behavior Based on Abstract Categories   95

5.3   Constructing the Field of Distributions in Space
(Configurations)   98

5.4   The Reference Matrix: A Definitive Instrument for the City
Planning Laboratory   100

5.5   Possible Interrelations among Histories   104

5.6   Possible Categories of Observable Activities and Their
Interpretations   107

6 THE CITY   110

6.1   The Private City   110

6.2   Problems Become Meaningful Only If We Have Adequate
Information: The Infrastructure as Medium   112

6.3   The Infrastructure Must Fulfill Certain Conditions   114

6.4   The Infrastructure Is Not the City   116

6.5   An Example of the Infrastructure as "Hardware": The
"Spatial City"   116

6.6   Modifying a Choice Carried Out within the Infrastructure   121

Appendix to Chapter 6: New Problems in the Industrialization of
Construction   124

7 SOME CONCLUSIONS ABOUT SOCIETY   128

7.1   The Noncompetitive Society   128

7.2   Crisis   132

Some Superficial Conclusions   135

APPENDIX: SOCIETY ⇋ ENVIRONMENT   142

A.1   Terminology   142

A.2   Critical Group   152

A.3   Critical Group and Environment   155

A.4   Realizable Utopias   158

A.5   Limited Effect of Technological Utopias   167

Conclusion   168

FOREWORD TO THE ENGLISH-LANGUAGE EDITION

In 1964, when I was a graduate student of architecture, I was sent to
the airport (because I spoke French) to pick up a visiting lecturer,
Yona Friedman. I was turned on by a soft-spoken but persuasive
argument for removing the architect as middleman between a user's
needs and their resolution in the built environment. Friedman's thesis
rested, in part, on the matter of who bore the risk in bad design. A
decade later, I find myself working with him (under National Science
Foundation support) and personally close to him and his ideologies.

For me the excitement in this volume results from its simplicity.
Yona Friedman has used a mathematical scaffolding to support philo-
sophical positions in a manner which affords the reader the opportunity to disagree with his utopian posture, but still benefit from his
techniques. I see this volume as an excellent example of scientific inquiry into design, so desparately lacking in our profession.

If you are a student of architecture you will find the paradoxical intersection of two academic streams—participatory design and scientific
methods—too frequently held apart by the circumstance of our train-
ing. You will find that Friedman contradicts the scholastic insinuation
that, if you can understand graph theory, for example, you probably
lack the human compassion and breadth of thought necessary to appreciate social goals. I believe that he offers the most genuine view of in-
dividualization and community development in architecture without
timidity and without political rhetoric.

If you are a practitioner of architecture you should expect to find
illustrations of the bitter conflict between good intentions and pater-
nalistic ideas of professional behavior. Nonetheless, Friedman provides
an early warning mechanism which is as applicable to the design of
airports and hospitals by professionals as the design of homes by
future users. His methods afford simple but essential predictions like:
This space must be small, this will have no light—without any commit-
ments to physical form.

If you are a researcher in architecture you can enjoy the exemplary
nature of this probe into the science of design. It epitomizes a style of
research that is based on personal experience and does not require the
paraphernalia of institutions and equipment.

This book is one result of Friedman's inquiry. For students, architects, and researchers, its benefits should derive even more from the questions raised than from the questions answered.

Nicholas P. Negroponte

PERSPECTIVE

Since 1957, I have been working on a theory which would free the client from the "patronage" of the architect, and at the same time, I have been looking for a way to make the architect useful to the client. This theory has introduced new terms (which I had to invent) such as "mobile architecture" and "spatial planning," and new techniques which I've worked out, such as "spatial infrastructure," a technique that allows maximum freedom to the inhabitant. The thesis which took shape from this theory was published in 1958 in mimeographed form and deposited in the Bibliothèque Nationale in 1959.

The propositions contained in this publication (and in the following ones) were poorly received by most professionals, but very quickly imitated by the most far-seeing ones—that is, the very good architects (young ones, as well as those who had already "arrived") such as Schulze-Fielitz (1961), Kenzo Tange (1962), Kurokawa, the Archigram group, Safdie, Bofill, Mühlestein and many others. I was personally very proud and flattered, although, for the most part, their works were too much inspired by the kind of visualizations (drawings or photographs of models) that have appeared in professional journals since 1959, journals which have published too many pictures without spending enough time on the reasoning which led me to these visualizations. For the most part, these architects also did not understand that the forms which I proposed were only the result of this very strict reasoning.

This book tries to provide some perspective by presenting nothing but the reasoning, without wandering off into visualizations of the results which this reasoning has produced.

The inevitability of this strict reasoning has had one direct consequence: many of my friends (and especially those I have named) have
had to come to the idea of "infrastructure," without completely understanding at what point it became inevitable . . . and it is, for it is the
only possible answer to the wish to emancipate the inhabitant, the only
possible conclusion from the idea that such an infrastructure should
not be too much a determinant of the chosen behavior of each inhabitant.

The fact that I can finally publish an architectural book that is nothing but reasoning—without worrying about pictures—is a clear sign that
the spirit of a generation of architects has changed: now, having imitated, it can learn why that imitation was commendable, being inevitable.

Yona Friedman
Paris, 1970

TOWARD A SCIENTIFIC ARCHITECTURE

CHAPTER 1 DEMOCRATIZATION

1.1 THE MANY

There are certain very important considerations of an epistemological nature at the basis of any scientific method. They give an idea of the subject it deals with and of the tools it employs and answer these questions: *what* can we know, and *how,* using these special tools, can we know it? In other words, these characteristics define the method by setting its boundaries.

It follows naturally from these statements that when the subject of a scientific method undergoes quantitative changes (and thus implicitly changes its boundaries) the method as a whole must be transformed. This is what has happened in physics, mathematics, and in biology and what is happening today in the behavioral sciences, including architecture and urban planning.

Before, the classic progression in architecture consisted of a simple chain of operations, which began with the future user of the architectural product (we will call him "user" or "client"). This client had very specific needs and personally conveyed them to the *architect.* The architect (or designer) drew up a plan *translating* the specific needs of the client into a piece of *hardware** which was supposed to fill those needs. The execution of the project was in the hands of a skilled tradesman. When the piece of hardware was finished, everyone was happy in the best of all possible worlds.

I have caricatured this process a little to underline the role of the architect as translator of the specific needs of the client into a lan-

---

*I use the word *hardware* here to mean the finished product, or building.

guage comprehensible to the skilled tradesman. The architect was an indispensable middleman as long as the client and the builder had no common idiom: there could be no doubt that at each stage of the process all the decisions had been made exclusively by the client.

At first sight the situation today seems to be identical, except for one factor, which is totally new: the number of clients has become enormous. But alas, our initial considerations have shown that a single new factor is more than enough to change the original situation completely, and that is what has happened.

In our crude representation, the client spoke directly with the architect about his specific needs. As it often happened that these needs were not very clear even in the client's mind, the architect had to devote a great deal of his time to acquiring sufficient information about them. I could cite as an example the famous architect who declared publicly: "In general, it takes about six months to understand one client's way of life,"

The question I ask is: How much time would he need to understand ten thousand clients?

Of course it is a purely rhetorical question. The time needed would be longer than the written history of mankind (which is about five thousand years). In spite of that, it is considered perfectly reasonable for today's architect or planner to work for ten thousand clients.

There are only two solutions to this problem:
1. Supply a large enough number of architects (or planners) so that each of them can devote himself to a very few clients.
2. Reduce the period spent gathering information (between the client's visit and the construction of the hardware.

The first solution would require unprecedented numbers of architects (it would amount to the creation of about two million architects in the next ten years, in the U.S.A. alone). Logically enough, the profession has chosen the second solution.

That is should have followed this course was bad enough, but the way in which it did so, which approached the absurd, was even worse. We shall see why.

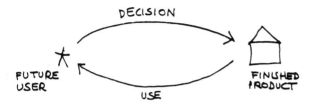

DECISION

FUTURE
USER

USE

FINISHED
PRODUCT

THE BASIC PROCESS INCLUDES
ONLY THE USER AND THE PRODUCT

Figure 1

The architects and planners said to themselves: It is impossible for us to find out out the specific needs of each user. Let's try to find out the average needs of future users, or, in other words, the *specific needs of the average future user.*

I do not think that it is necessary to describe the results in detail. It is enough to point to the massive discontent displayed by all users of architectural hardware. The reason for this discontent is evident: *the average client (user) does not exist.* Therefore, if all we do is satisfy the needs of the average consumer then logically we are not fully satisfying the needs of any of the real consumers. So instead of satisfying the real consumer, who does exist, we are satisfying one who doesn't.

Obviously this argument is simplified to prove the point. But the real situation is worse still: in my line of reasoning, I assumed that architects (or planners, or sociologists) were capable of objectively defining average needs. Now actually it was not just the logic of the notion that was fallacious; the very evaluation of the average user's needs was inevitably distorted by the preconceived ideas of those making it.

This critical situation results from a fact that the profession is trying to ignore, that is, that the number of clients has grown, which necessarily implies that the whole process of which the architect is a part must be changed.

The search for this new process is the object of this book.

1.2 INFORMATION PROCESSING: THE INFORMATION CIRCUIT BETWEEN USER AND PLANNER

Let us reconsider the situation. In the traditional process, as we have seen, the mechanism worked this way: the architect (or the planner) and the builder were only the "channel" by which "information content," or the "message," that is, the specific needs of the user, were relayed to the finished building.

This process was a simple one, made up of a *transmitting station* (the future user), a *channel* (the architect and the builder together), a *receiving station* (the hardware, or finished building), and information return or *feedback* (the usefulness of the product made available to the client). This system allowed for no corrections, no adjustments in case the feedback was unsatisfactory. Therefore, if the receiving station (the finished building) had not received the message (the specific needs of the client) from the transmitting station (the client), the responsibility lay with the channel (the architect and the builder). Any adjustments after the fact being impossible, the preliminary period, while the architect was getting to know the needs of his client, had to be very long indeed, as we have seen. As a consequence few or no modifications were necessary once the building was completed.

When this system was altered to serve an increased number of "future users" it became fundamentally different, as shown by the diagram in Figure 3.

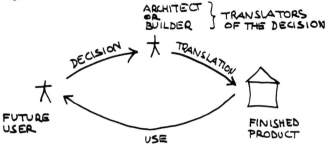

Figure 2

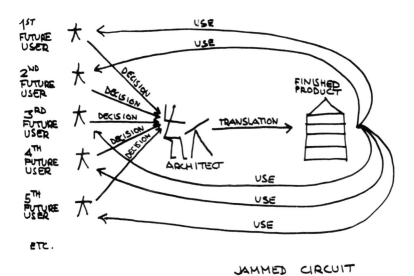

JAMMED CIRCUIT

Figure 3

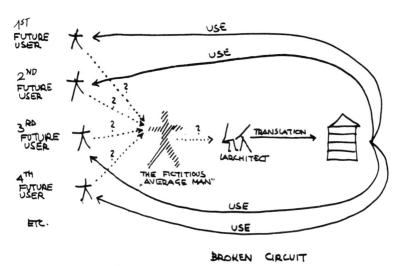

BROKEN CIRCUIT

Figure 4

The diagram shows the ideal situation as the architect and planner imagined it. Just for the sake of hypothesis, let's admit that this could work. The scheme has two bottlenecks: one at the architect's end and one at the point of actual construction. The first bottleneck is so narrow that it restricts the arrival of information to the architect; the second hinders feedback about the building once it is constructed. The vulnerable points of the system are these: the architect's handling of information, and the finished building's adjustment to uses as various as his client's.

The concept of the average man of course does not help the situation, since it merely adds a new step (and therefore new possibilities for error) without eliminating the bottlenecks. They stay the same, even though their positions are changed.

I shall call these two bottlenecks the architect's and planner's informational *short circuits.*

1.3 THE SOLUTION: DIRECT FEEDBACK FROM THE USER

Before continuing, I must try to define certain principles which I did not mention in the first section, principles which underlie all my reasoning so far.

Every science, every discipline or system, is essentially based on information. We can sum up the specific nature of a science or an art by defining the following points:

1. how (or by whom) the significant message was sent
2. how it was transmitted
3. the message which reached the recipient.

Epistemology is essentially information theory in disguise, and the decisive element in a discipline is the way it manipulates information in a given context. Naturally, when the context changes, the way of handling information must also change.

Now in the preceding section I stated that in the architectural process, there was one part of information handling (the channel) which had not changed as the context changed, so that the process had to readjust itself at another stage, involving the modification of the hardware for its uses. Unfortunately, this adjustment proved to be virtually impossible. That is the cause of the present crisis in the planning disciplines.

Our goal, therefore, is to construct a new process, which will eliminate information short circuits and therefore unreliability from the message on arrival, in other words, "noise" (disturbance in an informational system). The process would look something like Figure 5.

Figures 5 and 6 build on the relationship between two loops; neither one has a bottleneck like the ones in Figures 3 and 4.

The first loop represents the future user's direct decision. This loop includes only the user at one end, and, at the other end, a repertoire of all physically possible combinations of hardware he could bring about.

The second loop includes only the user of the finished product.

In these two loops, the intermediary—the role played by the architect or planner—has been eliminated. If it were necessary, we could put him back in the second loop to interpret between the client and the finished building (and thus act as artisan), but never in the first loop. We have eliminated the bottleneck which appeared in the diagram in Figures 3 and 4 by dividing the original loop into two separate ones. This operation allows us to line up, side by side, as many double loops as are necessary for as many users, because each loop is distinct along

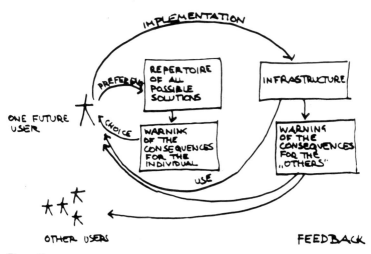

Figure 5

its entire course.

I shall explain the significance of Figure 6 by using the example of an imaginary but possible situation.

In our scheme, instead of an architect, the future user encounters a *repertoire of all the possible arrangements (solutions)* that his way of life may require. This repertoire, which is necessarily limited, must be presented to him *in a form he can understand.* Thus, for each item in the repertoire there is a warning. It tells the future user—again, in terms he will understand—the advantages and disadvantages, in terms of use, of picking a particular item. (The warnings, we will see in Chapter 3, are not based on any particular value system, but on the intrinsic properties and the logic of the projected solution; it may happen that the same warning can represent an advantage to one user and an inconvenience to another, since two clients may have entirely different ways of life.)

Thus, the first loop is the *user informing himself* by means of the repertoire. The way in which this repertoire may be put together is dis-

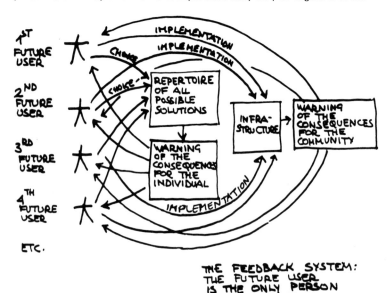

THE FEEDBACK SYSTEM:
THE FUTURE USER
IS THE ONLY PERSON
IN THE CIRCUIT

Figure 6

cussed in Chapters 2 and 3. We will describe how it is linked with a warning system in Chapters 3 and 4.

This first loop ends with the future user's choice of one item from the list in the repertoire.

The second loop resembles the classic process very closely; the future user explains his choice directly to the artisan, who will produce the building. To do this, the user indicates his choice by means of a number code, taken from the repertoire. The artisan (or the contractor) erects the hardware chosen (or conceived) by the client, who then puts the object of his choice to use. It is he who takes responsibility for the entire process, since he has been forewarned of the implications of the particular solution he has chosen.

In this remodeled version of the process, the two loops begin and end with the user: the first with his decision, the second with his communication of this decision and the results.

No special channel, no interpreter is necessary in these two loops. At first glance, it seems that the architect or the planner, who has for centuries kept his role as interpreter, has been eliminated from the process.

Actually it is a little different; in fact, the channel has not been eliminated in the new process. The channel is the repertoire itself, or, more precisely, the notation (mapping) used in the repertoire. This mapping must be understood by any user, as well as by the artisan who constructs the building. Thus the remodeled process takes us back to the scheme in Figure 1, which consists of three elements: the future user, the channel (in Figure 2 the architect, in Figure 5 the repertoire) and the finished product.

So it is really not the architect or planner who has been eliminated from the process, but rather his old role. He has a place, a new role, in the new system: *he constructs the repertoire.*

I am going to try to give an example of this process, an example taken from a system that does not involve the environment directly, so simple that we are not even aware that a scheme exists. It is the telephone system.

The repertoire: all the combinations of ten digits (in the United States). Any ten-digit number is a potential telephone number.

THE 2 AXES OF COMPETENCE

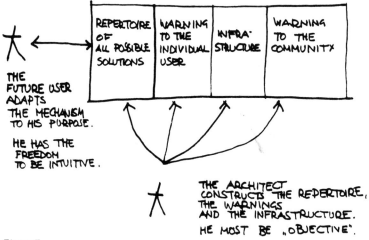

Figure 7

The warning to the individual: the telephone directory. It warns anyone who wants to make up a telephone number of the consequences of his act: it tells him who will answer his call.

The infrastructure: the technical network. This network, if it is constructed properly, can route *all calls, all conversations from any station to any other.* The telephone technicians have no obligation to tell you to whom you should speak or what you should say. *The infrastructure, therefore, is impersonal.*

Warning to the community: when you are on the line, your number and the number of your caller will be busy, so that any third person calling in will hear the busy signal.

Of course this example is very rudimentary; but it can point up how a highly technical and therefore impersonal system like the telephone can be used *to express the most personal feelings of the people who use it.* This example also shows that the task of technicians is not to deal with the emotional, intuitive aspect of use (in our example, the job of the technicians has nothing to do with the *content* of the conversations). Their job is to *establish the repertoire, the instructions, and the infrastructure.*

1.4 ARCHITECTURE: A "TEACHABLE" SCIENCE

Let us look at architecture in this new light: architecture, the design of complete repertoires that hold all the possible solutions to a problem, thanks to a specific notation (mapping) and the elaboration of a method which will match up a warning with each item in the repertoire.

This brief statement completely overturns the old image of architecture or planning, insofar as it still exists. To see what kinds of changes this will bring about in the profession, we can start by examining what kinds of equipment will be given to those who practice it.

Today there are no strict rules, either in architecture or in city planning, which allow us to predict accurately the results of a particular decision. Both professions make use of tricks of the trade. These tricks do not necessarily work in every case, and it is often difficult to tell the difference between a case where they will work and a case where they will not.

This observation implies that tricks cannot be taught without getting into awkward situations (because they are not generally applicable) and there is no method of imposing objective control by reference to context. A trick of the trade is basically a highly intuitive rule (see the first section of Chapter 2).

How do schools function when they deal with highly intuitive systems? Learning is dispensed by "masters," who have their own special tricks, which are usually impossible to communicate. Even though they can use them, they can't teach them. Masters are surrounded, therefore, by apprentices who do their best to imitate their master's working style, hoping by one means or another to pick up his "touch."

I call such disciplines the "prenticeable" disciplines. Here, the qualifications of the student depend essentially on the *qualifications or the personality of the master.*

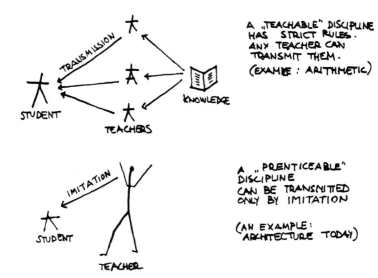

A „TEACHABLE" DISCIPLINE
HAS STRICT RULES.
ANY TEACHER CAN
TRANSMIT THEM.
(EXAMPE : ARITHMETIC)

A „PRENTICEABLE"
DISCIPLINE
CAN BE TRANSMITTED
ONLY BY IMITATION

(AN EXAMPLE:
ARCHITECTURE TODAY)

Figure 8

But there are other disciplines, for the most part called sciences, in which strict rules have been established, at least for the most important areas, rules which are valid in a well-defined set of instances. In these disciplines the entire system of rules is as generalized as possible.

In these disciplines, schools operate according to an arsenal of rules, which are available to the public (in books or films, for instance). Anybody who reads and understands these rules can apply them himself, without having to imitate the masters; and once he understands them, he can communicate them to anyone else. They are stated in such a way that in any instance it is clear whether they apply or not.

I call these the teachable disciplines. In these areas of study, the personality of the teacher is of no importance.

And so, if the activities of architects and planners today derive from learning by apprenticeship, their new work, as we have just seen, will emerge by contrast as a science that can be taught.

1.5 ARCHITECTURE CAN BE TAUGHT AT THE PRIMARY LEVEL

The point of such a long introductory chapter is to insist on this fact:

the power of choice rightfully belongs tc the future user. That is why
this chapter is entitled "Democratization," for the word *democracy*
indicates that everybody has his share in making the decisions (the elec-
tion of a plenipotentiary representative is no more than a very secondary, and a very distorted, form of democracy).

The act of deciding also implies that the one who makes the decisions
is the one who takes the risks. *Any system that does not give the right
of choice to those who must bear the consequences of a bad choice is
an immoral system.* But that is exactly the way that architects and
planners work. They make the decisions and the users take the risks.

To do away with this situation, I have looked for methods that will
guarantee to the future user the power of decision—*after he thoroughly
understands the risks involved.* It is both immoral and dangerous to
leave choices to people who have not been properly informed about
the consequences of their decisions.

The problem, which was initially one of information, is still one of
information, but on a different level. The important question is: How
do we inform the future user? (Information *is* politics, and the only
true form of politics.)

Let's look again at the example in Figure 5, where the future user
had to make a choice from a repertoire in which he found all the necessary instructions. To use this information (the repertoire and the instructions) *he had to be able to read both of them, but not to set them
up himself.*

The professional who sets up the repertoire and the instructions has to be
a scientist, practicing a teachable discipline. He will be the new version
of the architect or planner: the "redesigned" architect or planner.

The future user and the planner-scientist will need the same skills:
they must know how to read the repertoire, how to make choices from
it, and how to read the warnings. These are skills that should be taught
in primary school.

But the planner-scientist will have more to learn: "objective" rules and
their application to the construction of a repertoire and its warnings.
He will study these at the university level.

There is nothing unusual about this situation: mathematicians and lay-men use the same methods and the same rules, but on different levels. Anyone can read a weather map, but only a scientist can draw one.

The key to the functioning of an environment structured and ruled democratically rests in this twofold instruction.

We shall study both its aspects in the following chapters.

CHAPTER 2 ESSENTIALS OF THE METHOD

2.1. OBJECTIVE AND INTUITIVE SYSTEMS

In order to understand how to build a repertoire we have to examine the informational content of systems. (N.B. I use the term *system,* here and later on, to mean a set of elements where all the elements are linked (related) to the set by at least one link (relation) but where the links do not necessarily have any regularity. (Thus a structure, defined as a set of relations among the subsets of a set where the elements are put together according to particular rules, is implicitly a system, but a system does not necessarily have a structure).

Let's suppose that I had to describe a system so that other people could understand which one I was talking about. There are two ways to do it: the first way would be to give a certain number of instructions that form a sequence, organized so that any person, whatever his tastes, his culture, his race, his opinions, could carry out this sequence. Once it had been carried out, the result would be the same, no matter who the experimenter happened to be. I call this an objective, or scientific, system. Naturally, the proper sequence of steps would have to be laid out as precisely as possible.

For example:

First condition (implied): the experimenter is within the earth's field of gravity.

First step: he takes a glass in his hand.

Second step: he lets go of the glass a yard or more above the ground.

Third step: result: the glass falls.

Fourth step: secondary result: the glass could break (this possibility

depends on conditions that are not defined here, such as the material
and shape of the glass, the kind of floor, and so forth).

This secondary result will depend on conditions not specified, and we
shall pass over it unless it is more precisely defined.

The diagram in Figure 9 represents the essentials of such a process,
which is the general scheme for all experiments of this sort, where the
personality of the experimenter has no effect on the result.

It is easy to see that, as long as the result of such an experiment is
known, we can always reconstruct an excellent approximation of the
prescribed sequence of steps; but there is no way of determining from
the final result who the experimenter was.

The opposite of this kind of description, which I shall call an objective description and which makes use of a series of steps, is another
kind, which I shall call "intuitive."

In the intuitive description of a system, there is no series of steps, but
rather a symbol, used as a code. The symbol may be all there is to convey a message. It contains information that cannot be communicated
any other way (which is why a symbol is needed); and we can be almost
certain that each experimenter will understand the content of any one
symbol differently, depending on his taste, his culture, his race, and his
opinions.

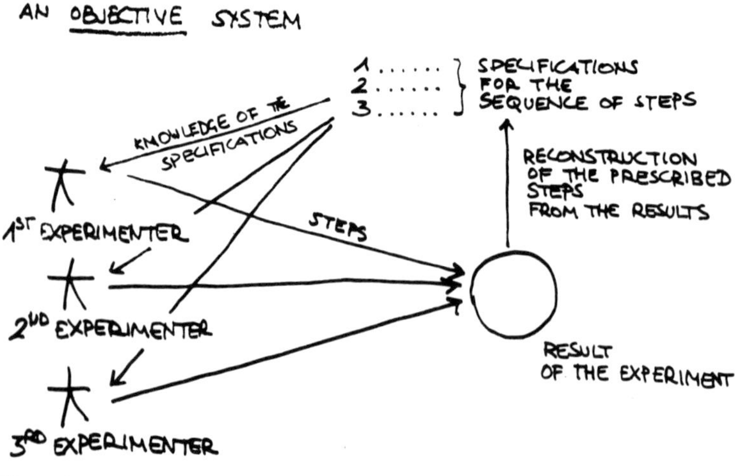

Figure 9

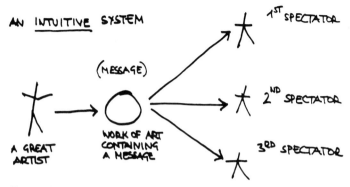

Figure 10

A good example of an intuitive system is art.

An artist creating a work of art considers that the message in his work is the important element, not the object itself. (According to my definition, a work of art is an object that carries a message). But in reality each spectator of an art object receives a different message; and if I know how the message is interpreted by one spectator (which in this example constitutes the result of the experiment) I will not be able to reconstruct the original message, but it will certainly give me a good idea of the personality of that particular spectator.

Clearly, this classification of ways of description has been simplified a great deal. In reality, there are no pure cases that belong exclusively to one of these methods. Any system can be described both ways, or, more exactly, it should be described both ways at the same time. However, we can say that a system is described largely by the objective method (and is thus an objective system) or largely by the intuitive method (and is thus an intuitive system). In their classic form, architecture and planning are intuitive systems.

The theme of the first chapter was that the situation in architecture and planning needs to change with respect to objectivity and intuition. I divided the discipline into two distinct parts; the part that concerns the planner has become an objective system, while the part that is intuitive involves the user, as shown in Figure 11.

So, from now on I shall consider only the objective part of the dis-

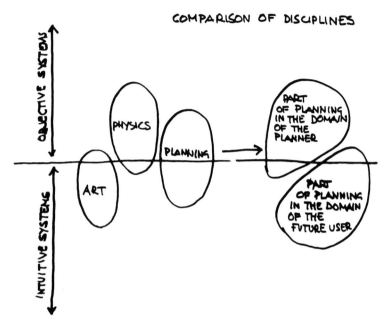

Figure 11

cipline, not because it is more important, but because it is the part that can be communicated, and the part that can be worked out. The repertoire that I am trying to establish must therefore be constructed as an objective system.

2.2 A COMPLETE LIST OF SOLUTIONS AS AN ACCEPTABLE ANSWER

We've seen that the specific criterion for defining an objective system is the possibility of reconstructing its "history" (the sequence of steps which led to a given and recognizable result). Therefore, we can extend the definition of objective systems to systems which are characterized by one or several series of steps, all of which can be reconstructed once the final result is known. (All sciences work this way.)

  Here I have to point out that for practical reasons the word "several," which I just used, necessarily represents a finite number in my mind. For if it also implied an infinite number, the criterion of "constructi-

bility" would not be respected. Infinity is only potential; and nobody
has ever been able to construct it.

Now to clarify the expression "one or several series," I am going to
try to give a simple example. Suppose I want to find out how a particular person arrived at the number 5 by adding two integers together.
It is unlikely that I could guess the way he actually did it, but I could
make a list of all the possible ways of doing this addition, and state that
whichever formula was actually used, it must be included in the following list: 0 + 5, 1 + 4, 2 + 3. These sums make up an exhaustive list.

If the question were: "How did someone get the number 5 by taking
the difference of 2 integers?" the problem would be fundamentally different. I could start the list: 5 − 0, 6 − 1, 7 − 2, and so forth, but since
it is infinite this second list would never be exhaustive, and I could
never state for sure that the formula actually used by this person was
on the list. Therefore, according to the criteria of objective systems, this
second list does not constitute an acceptable answer.

To continue this premise with a more general statement: if there are
two finite sets, A and B, the union of these sets (A ∪ B) satisfies the

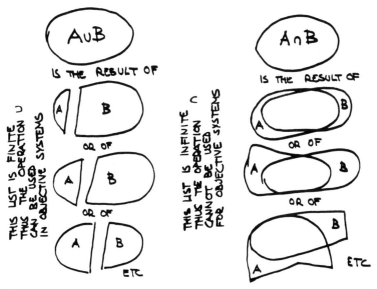

Figure 12

criteria of objective systems, but their intersection $(A \cap B)$ does not, for $A \cup B$ can be broken down into a finite list of all the possible combinations of A and B, whereas $A \cap B$ cannot (Figure 12).

2.3 CHOOSING AN APPROPRIATE AXIOMATICS

The preceding paragraphs were mostly concerned with the *conditions* for the description of a system, whatever it may have been. Now we come to the next problem: *how do you describe the system?*

Every description is made up of a number of statements. The number can be any finite number (a description made with an infinite number of statements is pointless, as we've already seen). If a system is made up of relations (links) and elements to start with, the number of statements that make up its description cannot be greater than the sum of the number of elements and the number of links. We could simply say that the most complete description of the system is the system itself.

Naturally the least complete description would be made by just one statement about it; for example: system X exists.

A description of a system must have at least a certain number of statements, the actual number being a positive integer somewhere between 1 and n, n standing for the number of elements plus the number of links.

If the system presents even the slightest regularity (if there is a structure, several similar elements or several similar connections between elements) the most complete description of the system will have several repeated statements. In order to simplify, we'll replace those repetitions with a new statement that indicates that statement S is repeated n times. If these repetitions recur regularly, we can say that each time condition C happens, statement S will be repeated.

All these statements, replacing the simple repetition of a series of identical statements, will allow us to reduce the number of statements we need to describe the system. Moreover, the list of statements that make up the description will be shorter. Statements displaying this regularity will be called systems of abbreviation. (I use this term and *structure* interchangeably.)

It is obvious that the abridged description is more convenient to use than the long one. It is also obvious that an abridged description, without losing its accuracy, does run the risk of being less complete than an unabridged one.

As for the characteristics of the statements making up a description, we could postulate the following: the statements must be clear to anyone; they must meet the criteria I have set down for objective systems; all their terms must be the "results" of a series of simple steps; and the results must be the same for anyone, that is, for anyone relying on a well-defined category of knowledge.

I shall call these statements axioms, and the terms of these statements primitive terms. Consequently, a system can be described by means of axioms. They will not be explained themselves (that is, described by means of other "meta-axioms"), but, given that they have been constructed as an objective system, they will be assumed to be universally understood, accepted, and verified.

These axioms must meet certain conditions:

1. An axiom cannot contradict the statement of another axiom used to describe the same system. (The axioms must be consistent.)

2. An axiom cannot repeat the statement made by another one that describes the same system (they must not be redundant).

3. Finally, all the axioms that are used to describe a system must be sufficient, taken together, for an approximate reconstruction of the entire system; that is, there must be no instance where an event (or term) belonging to the system does not have a place, even if under a collective noun, in the system of description (the axioms must be complete).

It is very difficult to fulfill these conditions, especially if there are too many axioms. Actually, these conditions convey the fact that the axioms describing a system are all interlinked.

When I state the first axiom, its content does not matter, and I am completely free to choose it arbitrarily. By contrast, I am no longer free at all in choosing the second one. It has to state a new fact, not covered by the first axiom, and it cannot contradict the first one. Therefore, I must limit my choice for the second axiom by verifying that it is both consistent and nonredundant with respect to the first. The process of solution will be the same for the third axiom, but more compli-

cated (because of the condition of nonredundancy and consistency
with respect to the first and second axioms), and so forth.

When I come to choose the last axiom, besides verifying that it is
nonredundant and consistent with respect to all the preceding axioms,
I have to verify whether an additional consideration is fulfilled and ask
myself: is the description of the system complete enough to satisfy its
purpose? For it is the purpose which determines the degree of simplification—or abbreviation—of the description.

To describe this process of verification, I should say that each axiom
must close back on the preceding ones. Once the axiomatics is complete, I will no longer be able to tell which axiom was the first in the
series of operations (the order of construction of the axiomatics); the
axioms should close back on each other, whatever order they are listed
in.

An axiomatics (a system of axioms) is, therefore, a completely closed
system, in which all the links represent the same primitive generating
steps. The (entire) system therefore consists of the same primitive terms.

I now propose to use a device: let us represent an axiomatics graphically in the following way. A point will represent an axiom, a line joining two points will be a link, and an arrow on the line will show which
axiom comes after which. We shall think of these diagrams (mappings)
as plane figures (no line can pass over another). The graphic one-to-one
representation (mapping) of a system containing n axioms will be
shown by a *complete planar n graph.*

Figure 13 shows that everything goes well in a system of axioms as
long as it includes no more than three axioms; all the conditions (consistency, nonredundancy, and closure) can be verified. The trouble
starts with the fourth axiom. The last line, that of closure, has an arrow
whose direction cannot be determined without additional information
on the subject described by the system. So the axiomatics is not necessarily complete. In other words, it is impossible to verify consistency,
nonredundancy, and closure for the lines of a system of four axioms
without introducing an additional statement.

There are even more difficulties in a system of five axioms. In such a
system, the problem is not the direction of the arrow (this occurs only

A SET OF n ELEMENTS
CAN BE DESCRIBED BY STATEMENTS
ANYWHERE FROM 1 TO n IN NUMBER

IF A STATEMENT IS REPRESENTED BY   •
A RELATION BETWEEN 2 STATEMENTS BY   ——
AND THE ORDER IN WHICH THE STATEMENTS FOLLOW
EACH OTHER   BY   ——→

THEN A SYSTEME OF n ELEMENTS
CAN BE DESCRIBED BY STATEMENTS AS FOLLOWS :

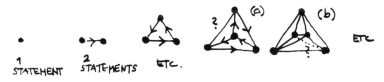

•   •→•
1   2
STATEMENT   STATEMENTS   ETC.   ETC.

(a) IN THE CASE OF 4 STATEMENTS
    THE ORDER IN WHICH THEY FOLLOW EACH OTHER
    CANNOT BE EASILY ESTABLISHED

(b) MORE THAN 4 STATEMENTS RESULT IN A "CROSSOVER",
    THUS THEY IMPLY AN UNENUNCIATED
    ADDITIONAL STATEMENT.

Figure 13

when n is an even number). Here, there appears a crossover which is
not authorized by our mapping, for its literal significance would be that
of an unstated axiom; our system of five axioms would become an
incomplete system of six axioms, which we cannot allow becuase of its
character of incompleteness.

A complete n graph will always have crossovers when n is equal to or
greater than five. So a system of five or more axioms will always run
the risk of being incomplete.

This little exercise tells us (if the mapping was correct) that an axiomatic description with more than three axioms would be vulnerable
(with respect to consistency, nonredundancy, and closure) in every
case where an experimental verification of the original system (which
was the point of the description) is unfeasible.

One could ask: is mapping a system of axioms by means of a complete planar graph really a proper one-to-one representation? For example, could not the problem of the crossovers be eliminated by using a nonplanar graph for the mapping?

Mapping with planar graphs is, in fact, perfectly correct; for if we were to allow nonplanar solutions, we would need an additional rule which explained the significance of the additional dimension in setting up the graph, a rule which in itself would have no representational value.

Each element in the mapping (points, lines, labels) has a clearly defined significance. But this rule of the additional dimension would have none, so it would represent a foreign element which would correspond to nothing in the system.

On the other hand, our mapping system does not exclude systems of three or more dimensions; it only discourages them, because the absence of a statement explaining the significance of an additional dimension makes unworkable (incomplete) systems.

There follows this simple precept, on which I shall rely throughout this work: the description of a system of axioms is most convenient (easiest to verify with respect to consistency, nonredundancy, and closure) when there are no more than three axioms.

These three axioms can be easily constructed as follows: the first identifies the system to be described by naming the operations at the origin of the system; the second imposes a restriction (specification) on the first, and the third restricts both the first and the second. For example, we can take the step-by-step description of the mechanism of comprehension as a basic model for this kind of axiomatic system.

The first step in every process of human comprehension consists of the identification of something. Let us think of this identification as putting a mental label on that something so that it will be possible to tell if it is or is not the thing we have labeled.

The second step consists of delimiting (of setting apart) the thing labeled from all the other things. The labeled thing will be thought of as unique.

The third step consists of making a comparison between the labeled thing and all other things.

I shall call these steps:
1. identification (of one thing among others)
2. establishing uniqueness (of the labeled thing)
3. establishing a relation (between the labeled thing and all other things).
  Even if this system, and particularly this example, is a little off the path I have decided to follow in order to discover a science of planning, it is necessary to take the detour, because it will be useful later on.

2.4 AXIOMS TO DESCRIBE THE WORK OF ARCHITECTS AND PLANNERS
In this essential section we can finally leave the realm of abstract reasoning and come back to questions of professional concern for architects and planners. I shall apply the preceding argument to this realm, first of all in trying to find an axiomatic description, as general as possible, for the work of these professions.

  The general description includes three statements, in accordance with a previously fixed condition. This previous condition will not, properly speaking, be part of the axiomatics itself, but it will determine its range of validity. (I have said that any operational result must be valid for anyone, that is, any person belonging to a well-defined category).

  The range of validity for our axiomatics will be any space where a human being can physically survive (in practical terms, what we call the biosphere).

  The work of architects and planners deals with effecting separations within the biosphere. In fact, if we examine any product made by an architect or planner, we can state that it takes the form of an "envelope," or an "enclosure." The interior of this envelope encloses a volume or a surface separated from the exterior. The fundamental task of the planner as well as of the architect is the activity of making this separation. The only difference is that the first works on two-dimensional envelopes like zones while the second builds three-dimensional envelopes. But both activities produce enclosures.

  So the first axiom will be: the work of architects and planners produces enclosures—separations in space.

  But there are many kinds of enclosures that are not products of the

architect's or planner's skill, because they are inaccessible. They are
things such as boxes, sardine tins, and the empty spaces inside objects.
So it will be practical to choose a second axiom that can state this
specification: a separation of space (an enclosure) cannot be the work
of architects and planners if it does not have at least one access. In
other words, any two spaces separated by an architect or a planner
must have at least one "path" linking them.

When architects or planners bring about separations in space, they
do it so that the new spaces will all be given different qualities. The
act of enclosing creates differentiation. For example, an enclosure
could have climatic or visual qualities that are very different from
those of the original exterior biosphere or those of another enclosure.

So I shall propose a third axiom: in a system of spatial separations
there must be at least one enclosure that differs from the others in
some respect, whether as a result of physical qualities or of others.
Thus the three axioms I propose are:

1. Architects and planners bring about separations in preexisting space.

2. Each of the separated spaces must have at least one access.

3. There must be at least two different kinds of separated space.

Without contradiction or redundancy, these three axioms describe
every step that architects and planners could think of. Therefore, this
axiomatics is complete.

Many people would be quick to point out that these axioms are trite.
But axioms have to be so by definition, for they must state a fact that
is acceptable to everyone, that is obvious, and so on. What is important
about the use of these axioms is that they allow for any solution imaginable proposed by any human being imaginable within the realm that
they define, except for those that are physically impossible.

2.5 A MAPPING FOR ARCHITECTS AND PLANNERS

By themselves, the axioms formulated in the preceding section are
not enough help: I could not actually construct a repertoire based on
them. To obtain the repertoire (the complete list of all the possible
solutions for one problem) we would have to set down all the solutions
in one way or another and then put the list in some kind of order. (The

list has to be in order so that we can find any item on the list whenever we need it. For example, we might use an alphabetical order, just as the telephone directory does. In that case, the rule which determines precedence, or which item comes after which, would be the rule of the alphabet.)

So the first problem we confront is which terms to include in the list, without leaving any out and without repeating. To arrive at this list, we shall apply the process of mapping, using a model which easily gives us a general view, and where each element corresponds to an element in the original system and only to that element (a one-to-one relationship). This relationship must hold for all the links among the elements in the two systems. Since the axioms cover both the elements of a system and the relationships among the elements, there is the same one-to-one relationship between the rules which determine the mapping and the axioms of the system represented by the mapping. We shall first try to determine the rules of the mapping. Once these rules are defined, we shall construct a combinatorial list of all the images that the rules of the mapping generate. And this list will correspond, element by element, to the repertoire which we wish to establish.

The term *mapping* indicates that there is a code which enables us to transcribe each step or element of the system represented (mapped), into a step or element of the system which represents it (mapping), and that in each of these two systems there is only one element which corresponds to any element in the other system. The mapping procedure lets us execute any step at all on the map, and to transpose this step into the real system. So there is a *real* result which corresponds to the results of each mapped step, and we can recognize the real result by comparing the result obtained on the map.

Now I am going to introduce a mapping code, which will be a code of connected and labeled planar graphs, and we shall transcribe the axioms into the rules of the mapping.

First axiom: a separated space can be created inside a preexisting space.

First rule: there is a point to represent the preexisting space, and each enclosed space in the preexisting space is represented by another point.

Therefore, any graph that represents an enclosed space has to contain at least two points.

Second axiom: an enclosure has at least one possible access from another enclosure, and there can be no enclosure that is inaccessible from some other enclosure.

Second rule: a line represents an access. This line links the points representing the two enclosures joined by the access. In any figure, there must be no single point without at least one line to the other points.

Third axiom: there are at least two different kinds of enclosures of which one is the preexisting space.

Third rule: there is a label to represent each category of enclosure. In each representative figure, there are at least two labels (one for the preexisting space and one for the enclosures).

These three rules constitute a complete mapping for the axiomatic system which relates to the activities of architects and planners. They allow us to construct a list of every possibility. The mapping is made up of points and lines, arranged so that every point or group of points is linked to all the other points. All these points carry labels, and the labels are of at least two kinds (planar graphs, connected and labeled).

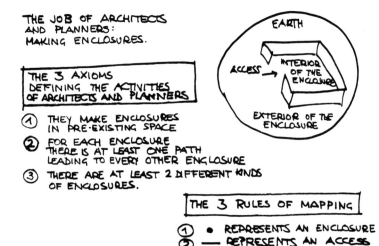

Figure 14

Some people will inevitably object to this axiomatic description, along with its corresponding mapping rules, as being a little simplistic . This would clearly be wrong; in fact, the description of the axioms and the rules of the mapping cover every imaginable physical possibility for joining enclosures together, and, thanks to the use labels, the enclosures or their connections can be as different or as alike in any respect as we are capable of imagining them.

The system I am proposing here is richer (offers more combinations) than anything architecture has produced to date, in all of human history. And if one thinks about the variety of repertoires that can be built by means of this mapping, one is amazed at the results, seeing the poverty of our imagination.

2.6 CONSTRUCTING COMBINATORIAL LISTS
Now we come to our goal: the setting up of repertoires.

First of all, in this section we shall look at the abstract model for constructing lists, and study the question of which rules must be respected. All of Chapter 3 will deal with translating these abstractions into reality.

The mapping which we have decided on uses planar graphs, connected and labeled, each corresponding to a particular plan taken from the list of possible plans.

Every list of graphs will be composed as a function of n, n being the number of points contained in the graph (that is, the number of enclosures in the plan).

Actually, there is no algorithm for the construction of such a list. Therefore we will proceed (manually or with the help of a computer) with the induction of a new point into the list of known ones.[*]

Just as an example, we shall construct all the solutions (and therefore all the graphs) for $n = 2$, $n = 3$, $n = 4$. We'll only use two labels in these examples: the sign O, representing exterior preexisting space, and the sign 1, representing the interior of a separated space. In this way there will only be one sign O on every graph, all the other labels being 1.

---

[*]I call "construction by induction" the construction of a complete list of $(n + 1)$ graphs, obtained by adding a point outside the graph to each possible n graph, and by linking this point in every possible way to the points of each n graph.

THE RULES OF MAPPING PERMIT
CONSTRUCTION OF COMPLETE COMBINATORIAL LISTS
OF ALL POSSIBLE SOLUTIONS

2 ENCLOSURES HAVE ONLY 1 POSSIBLE LINKAGE

3 ENCLOSURES HAVE 3 POSSIBLE LINKAGE SCHEMES

4 ENCLOSURES HAVE 11 POSSIBLE LINKAGE SCHEMES

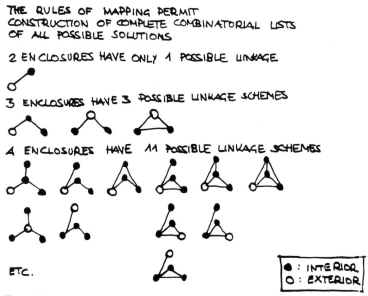

ETC.

●: INTERIOR
○: EXTERIOR

Figure 15

There are eleven figures in the complete mapping list for $n = 4$, these
figures being included in the list only when they are topologically different from the others (when a figure cannot be transformed into another by the distortion of its links, without cutting them, as if, for example, the graphs were made of wire, and could be bent in any direction without changing the pattern or linkage scheme according to which
they are joined). They could also be represented in a more convenient
visual arrangement, where the label O would be replaced by a white dot.

I could also establish this list by using, instead of graphs, their adjacency matrix. By this I mean a binary matrix which will show by the
symbol 1 if, between two points, noted one at the head of a column,
the other at the beginning of a row on the matrix, there is an immediate link (adjacency) and will show by 0 if there is no immediate link.

The adjacency matrix is always symmetrical with respect to the principal diagonal when the links do not have a directional arrow, that is
when each link permits movement in either direction. On the other

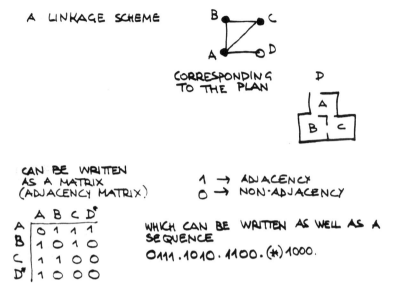

A LINKAGE SCHEME

CORRESPONDING TO THE PLAN

CAN BE WRITTEN AS A MATRIX (ADJACENCY MATRIX)

$1 \rightarrow$ ADJACENCY
$0 \rightarrow$ NON-ADJACENCY

	A	B	C	D*
A	0	1	1	1
B	1	0	1	0
C	1	1	0	0
D*	1	0	0	0

WHICH CAN BE WRITTEN AS WELL AS A SEQUENCE

0111.1010.1100.(*)1000.

* DENOTES A LABEL DIFFERENT FROM THE OTHERS (EXTERIOR SPACE)

Figure 16

hand, if a graph has directional arrows, the corresponding matrix is not symmetrical.

The difference between different graphs rests only in the position of the label O. Therefore we can put this sign in parentheses (O) before the element of the sequence which represents the location of the point marked O. In the preceding example, 0111 represents the point A, 1010 the point B, 1100 represents C, and 1000 represents D. Therefore for the same graph we could write the position of the point marked.O

the point O in A: 0111.(0)1010.1100.1000 or 0111.(0)1010;1100.1000
the point O in B: 0111.1010.(0)1100.1.000 or 0111.1010.(0)1100.1000
the point O in C: 0111.1010.1100.(0)1000 or 0111.1010.1100.(0)1000

In these notations, both the first and second expressions are exact, for the points in them represent a complete row or column of the matrix corresponding to the point in question.

What is important in these matrix notations is that they constitute a representation of the graph in computer language, and as we must rely on a computer to set up all large lists, it is advantageous to adopt a notation that does not have to be transcribed especially for it.

The combinatorial list of eleven figures (or matrices) in our example contains all the possible solutions for linkages among any four elements, as long as three of the elements have similar properties and there is no more than one with different properties.

It is impossible to imagine any solution not included in this list, and any other solution would be physically impossible. Therefore, this list of eleven solutions to the problem is complete, or exhaustive.

It goes without saying that it is also a complete list of solutions for establishing connections among four regions or four enclosures, where one is different from the other three.

I am sorry to say that I have often shown so-called analyses of architectural or planning problems worked out by professionals, and that in these analyses, which claim to compare possible solutions, certain solutions were always purely and simply overlooked, even though sometimes the solutions that were overlooked were precisely the ones that would have been most effective. Truly, sometimes our imagination is limited!

CHAPTER 3 THE NEW TASK OF ARCHITECTS AND PLANNERS

3.1 LIKE EATING OUT

The first two chapters described the problems of architecture and planning and proposed a solution based on the use of a repertoire. They also showed how it would be possible to build a repertoire, at least in the abstract. Now we're going to see how a repertoire would actually work.

Let us take an everyday example. Restaurants the world over organize their service in terms of a repertoire. We call that repertoire the *menu.*

The menu contains a list of all the dishes that the restaurant serves (these are the preexisting elements). The menu lists each dish by its name, along with a short description of how it is prepared and an indication of its price. We shall call the information accompanying each item on the list the *warning.* The warning tells the client what the consequences will be if he chooses a particular item on the list. In a restaurant, there will be economic consequences (involving the client's purse) or perhaps digestive consequences (involving his stomach). So if he has taken the trouble to read the menu, the client is well informed.

Next, he will put together a combination of different dishes—in other words, a meal. Probably no two clients will choose exactly the same combination, even if they are having dinner together. A meal is a matter of taste and personal choice, and there is no such thing as an independent scale of values that says one gastronomical composition is better than another one either in the absolute or on a scale of values.

The owner of the restaurant never interferes in the choice his client makes, whatever it is, even if the choice disagrees with his own personal taste, or if he thinks the bill will be extravagant. His job is to serve the client, whatever he has ordered from the repertoire, and in accordance with the information it contains. Actually, the restaurant owner's creative work lies in setting up the menu.

This example demonstrates the method that I propose for setting up a repertoire for the architect's client to use. The repertoire will be made up of a complete list of all the possible linkages and labeling (the *mapping* of the problem itself). The client (earlier we called him the future user) will actually have the freedom to choose any possible combination instead of having to go along with the preferences of some architect or other.

For each possible combination, the repertoire will have a corresponding warning indicating its cost. The warning will tell the client the cost expressed in *effort*; this is the intrinsic property of each combination, that is, the advantages or inconveniences of this combination in terms of the client's particular mode of use.

There is a third problem to be solved, to which the architect or planner must find a solution: again as with the restaurant, he must provide the support for all the possible combinations which a client is apt to want. The architect guarantees the hardware, or the *infrastructure*, in such a way that after the client has made a choice, he has the chance to change or modify his choice (and consequently change the corresponding hardware) when he thinks it desirable (see Sections 3.5, 3.6).

This example of the restaurant exactly describes the problems of architects and planners.

The restaurant does not take into account one element, however, that is very important for the architect: the fact that the warning given by the architect or planner must be addressed not only to the particular client who makes the choice, but also to the community (by means of media, for example).

In effect, the community must be informed *of the immediate consequences for it of every individual choice.*

The following sections of the chapter will deal with the menu in architecture, and Chapters 4 and 5 will deal with a method for informing the community about the consequences of individual choices.

3.2 BUILDING THE REPERTOIRE

Now let us set up the menu: the list of choices from which anyone can
make his own environment. This is the repertoire we have talked about
so often in the preceding chapters.

The basis for the repertoire will be the complete list of diagrams of
possible combinations, which we spoke about in Chapter 2. These combinations will be described by planar n graphs, connected and labeled
by means of $n - 1$ (at most) labels of one kind, and one label (at least)
of another kind; they correspond to the possibilities of arranging
$(n - 1)$ spaces which connect, directly or indirectly, with the exterior.

Elsewhere in connection with the rules of mapping I defined a label
as representing a *specialization* of space, a *difference*. It goes without
saying that the label, as it marks a difference, can indicate completely
heterogeneous categories, depending on a given context (country, social
class, technical methods, language, and so on) in which the architect
supposedly works. Just to demonstrate, let us establish a code of
labeling valid in a context chosen at random. The first important

AN EXAMPLE OF NOTATION

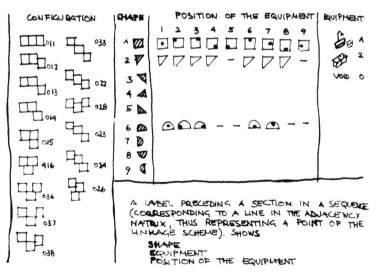

Figure 17

decision will concern what hierarchy one wishes to establish among the different categories. This hierarchy could be completely different for each individual, and it is thus subjectively established. For example, let us choose the labeling in Figure 17.

A point on the graph which carries the label 100 represents a square room, not equipped in any particular way. A line joining two points (which represent two rooms) and carrying the label 2 indicates that the squares representing the volumes overlap by half a side.

Let us take one of the graphs in Figure 15, for instance, the last one. We will give it an arbitrary label: Figure 18.

In a repertoire of solutions which deal with three rooms joined together and having specialized functions in accordance with the labeling of Figure 16, there are 11 possible basic combinations, (linkage schemes) and, for each combination, 15 labels for the kind of their linkage to each other, 18 for the shape of the rooms, 368 positions for 2 kinds of equipment (kitchen and bathroom); and each apartment can have 64 different orientations. The "menu" that started with a single set of labeling in fact contains $11 \times 15 \times 18 \times 368 \times 2 \times 64 = 24,330,240$ solutions in all.

Obviously that is an astronomical number (I hope that I have not made a mistake in calculating it; I am not very good at arithmetic). But this number does represent every possible solution for arranging these three rooms when one can choose, for each room, from three different shapes, two kinds of utilities, three positions, and four orientations. If you wanted to write out this list, it would take two hundred and forty volumes of a thousand pages, at a hundred lines a page (please see the parenthetical note in the preceding sentence).

This figure shows, once again, what meager intuitive proposals architects actually make. These 24 million solutions are *all that are possible, and all that could be desirable to a particular client.* And no one could decide ahead of time, without knowing this particular client, which solution he would personally choose.

The difficulty with such a voluminous list lies not only in the fact that the architect has practically no chance of guessing which solution a client will choose; the other trouble is that the client would certainly

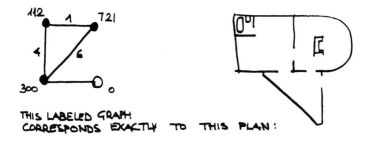

THIS LABELED GRAPH
CORRESPONDS EXACTLY TO THIS PLAN:

IT COULD ALSO BE WRITTEN
IN THIS SEQUENCE:

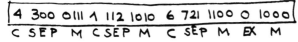

C: ARRANGEMENT
S: SHAPE
E: EQUIPMENT
P: POSITION OF E.
M: MATRIX LINE
EX: EXTERIOR

Figure 18

not know how to manage such an unwieldy catalogue in order to choose
his three rooms.

To make a choice possible, it would be useful to reduce the list, and
instead of using labels with five digits (representing the five categories)
to use an abridged list which would still be nonetheless complete.

We will make up a complete list where each label belonging to a point
on the graph would have just one digit. We could consider, just as an
example, the linkage of the rooms and their utilities, and ignore the
arrangement, the shape, the orientation, and so on. Then, the list of
labels, with each label corresponding to an appropriate set of equipment, could be the following:

1: kitchen + void, 2: bathroom + void, 3: void + void, 4: bathroom
+ kitchen.

If in our example we allow for no apartments without utilities, and

no apartments with two kitchens (and consequently admit that label
3 is the only one we would meet more than once in a given solution)
there are only six different ways to arrange each apartment: 123, 132,
231, 334, 343, 433. In certain graphs for the list of combinations, there
could be labels identical to each other because of the symmetry of the
graph (in these cases, the labels would be topological equivalents).
Indexes of the graphs in the list in Figure 15: 4 enclosures (3 rooms
plus exterior):   1 2 3 4 5 6 7 8 9 10 11
Number of possible combinations of labels: 6 6 5 6 6 6 6 6 6 5

The total of all the solutions (which covers, in less detailed form, the
24 million solutions which we mentioned before) will not exceed 64.
This list could be presented on a single page, and it constitutes a perfectly usable "menu."

Instead of reducing the number of labels, another way to present such
long lists is to give only the labels, with the rules of composition to be
applied to them, leaving all the real work and the decisions to the client.
The methods are essentially identical. The only difference lies in how
the list as a whole is presented.

In Section 7 of this chapter, we shall see a working example of the
second method, thanks to the use of a very simple machine which
makes things easier for the client.

I should add here a remark to explain why I only use planar graphs
(I have already explained a similar choice with respect to the axiomatics). A nonplanar graph is a graph of five or more points—we shall
come across one later on—which, on paper, will show crossovers. But
these crossovers (crossing points) do not conform to our rules, and
they have no meaning by our conventions, according to which a point
represents a space or an enclosure. We might consider the crossovers
as representing spaces or enclosures not catalogued in the repertoire of
enclosures, such as hallways or stairs.

There is a general statement which indicates, for a graph, the greatest
number of real connections that it can contain (the saturation point of
the graph): $L = 3(n - 2)$, where L represents the number of connections.

Every time the number of connections in the n graph is greater than L

there are inevitably crossovers, that is, spaces not catalogued in the repertoire of enclosures (in the set of enclosures mapped by the graph).

We find a typical example of a crossover, or an uncatalogued space, in the solution of a small, insignificant problem like the following: construct four rooms, each one of which is directly connected to each of the others and all having an access directly on a garden (Figure 19). However I try to plot this graph, there will inevitably be a crossover (C), which could be interpreted as representing a stairway or a corridor. Without the intervention of this sixth "uncatalogued" room, the problem is insoluble.

Now let us recapitulate the steps we take to construct the complete list of solutions for assembling n elements (the first part of our repertoire, without the instructions):
1. Construct the set of all the planar n graphs.
2. Choose positive categories in order of importance (according to personal and arbitrary criteria of appreciation) and rank each of the categories.
3. Assign a symbol as a label to each possible case in each category.

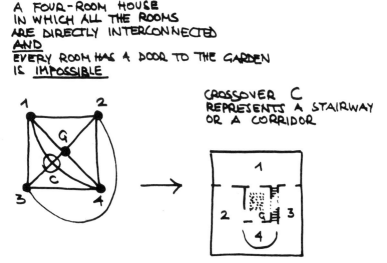

Figure 19

4. Set up all the possible labels according to the directions in steps 2 and 3.

5. Set up the complete labeling system for planar n graphs, using the labels established in step 4.

3.3 THE PATH MATRIX

As I have described it, the repertoire contains more than just a complete list of items. There is also a warning for each item catalogued in the repertoire, which is made up of two elements: the first is simply the purchase price (or the "purchase effort") for the combination in question. The second element indicates the characteristics of the hardware which corresponds to this number on the list—what the user can expect from it (tentatively, we will call this element the *use efficiency*).

The *path matrix* (which will be important in indicating the use efficiency of an item) shows the shortest distance from one point to another, for each pair of points on the graph. Like the adjacency matrix, it is symmetrical with regard to the principal diagonal for any graph which does not carry a directional arrow.

The $\sum d$ column shows the sum of all the distances from one point given on the n graph to all the other points on the same graph. $\sum d$, therefore, shows the average position of a given point ($\sum d/n - 1$ will be the term for the average distance from one point on the n graph to all the other points). Thus $\sum d$ can be used to measure the site advantage which a given room has in comparison to the other rooms within the same layout. In the example in Figure 20, I did not assume different distances between any two adjacent points, and to make matters simpler I proposed distances having the same length. In this example, enclosure C has a "privileged" site compared to rooms A and B, which, in turn, are privileged compared to room D.

But let us suppose that for his own reasons the future user does not use these four basic rooms equally. Let us suppose, for example, that in one day he were to go twice as often into room A as into rooms C and D, and three times as often into room B as into rooms C and D. We would call this frequency of movement to a particular room the *use weight* of that room, calculated for a given time span.

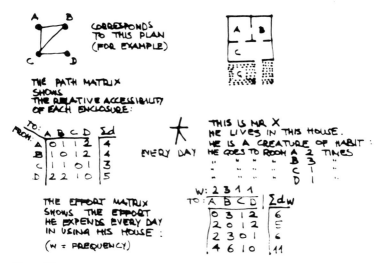

Figure 20

We could write the use weight into the series representing a graph, just as we did for the labels; for instance, we might write it in parentheses in front of the element in the sequence that represents a given point. So if you indicated the use weight that way, the graph in Figure 20 would give the following sequence:

(2) 110 (3) 110 (1) 111 (1) 001

Now let us construct the path matrix in an improved form. Each term of the new matrix will show the product *dw* of the distance by the use weight (or how often the route is used) for any two points. This product is obtained by multiplying the frequency of use (*w*) from the point which is the terminus of the path.

To obtain the new matrix, we write in above the path matrix, in the column which corresponds to each terminal point, the use weight of that point, and we multiply each term in the column (representing the distance) by this frequency (*w*). The matrix thus obtained will show the real effort the future user will make during a given time span (in this case, during one day) in using the set of enclosures in his particular way. This new matrix will be called the *detailed effort matrix* for this linkage of enclosures (apartment) or for the corresponding graph.

After constructing the detailed effort matrix, we shall take the sum of all the terms in each row of the matrix. The sum total of a given row corresponding to a point of departure on the graph (and to a given enclosure in the apartment), or the *local effort value,* will measure the site advantage of that enclosure within a given linkage scheme used in a particular way. The formula for local effort value (*E*) for the *n* graph will be:

$$E_x = \sum_{y=1}^{y=n} d_{xy} \cdot w_y$$

This formula represents our *warning system.* It makes it possible to inform the future user what the consequences will be if he chooses a particular linkage and uses it in his particular way.

To improve "readability," whenever the graph representing the set of enclosures has a large number of points, we shall indicate the local effort values *E* by writing them above each of the points that they belong to. We shall call these lines the *lines of isoeffort,* and the resulting map, the *map of isoefforts,* or the *effort diagram.*

To give an ideal of how this diagram works, let us suppose that the future user chooses the linkage of enclosures that he prefers. Once he has made the preliminary choice, he assigns to each enclosure in the set a use weight (*w*), reflecting his own way of using a particular room. The diagram constructed from these data (the linkage scheme and the "projected" use) will show the local effort value corresponding to each element in the set, as a function of the client's particular behavior.

So the effort diagram informs the future user about the consequences of his choice (comfort, physical exertion, and so on) and lets him compare these with the consequences of other preliminary choices he has made, until he decides on one of the linkages, the one that seems likely to give him the most satisfaction.

The effort diagram lets him experiment, in his mind, with several possible arrangements of space without having actually to build them all (which would be impossible in any case). It lets him compare different linkages from the point of view of a particular manner of use, whatever it may be, without making the mistakes usually made in intuitive comparisons. (Anyone who has served on an architectural jury knows that there is no common scale of values that would allow for a comparison of two projects, which is not true if one uses "effort maps").

It is very easy to construct this matrix, even without the help of a computer (as long as there are not a large number of points), and it provides useful information about the consequences of each choice, or of a change in a client's behavior.

In addition to local effort, later on we will also apply the concept of global effort, under the formula $e = \sum E = \sum \sum d$, which represents the sum of all the local efforts in a given linkage scheme for a given distribution of use weights. This concept will be very useful to us when the problem takes the form of a comparison, pure and simple, among different distributions of use weights within the same linkage, or among a large number of different linkages (Chapter 4).

3.4 THE SUPPORTING NETWORK AND ITS HARDWARE COUNTERPART

Everything discussed so far concerns only the act of choice. Who must make the choice, and why? What is a repertoire? How should a repertoire be built, and who should build it? What are the consequences of a choice between the possible alternatives? We have dealt with such questions as these.

Now, in this section and in Chapter 6, which covers the technological considerations, we come to the following problem: what is the "hardware" that makes it possible to construct any of the combinations in the repertoire with the minimum of constraints?

Let us examine the characteristics which we must look for in this undetermined hardware, which is necessitated by the fact that the actual construction, in the material sense of the word, cannot wait for the final decisions of all the future users, and cannot be delayed by long fruitless inquiries.

We have to find a kind of hardware that can be built before all the choices are made, and which, once they are made, allows for any organization of rooms according to a particular choice, whatever it may be.

We have already seen that individual choices were represented by points, lines, and labels, and that we could obtain a complete list of all possible choices by using these simple components and taking the following steps:

1. Take a set of n points
2. Make a combinatorial list of all the planar connections transforming the n points into a unique and closed figure
3. Construct for each of these links the combinatorial list of all possible m labels (m = the number of labels).

Actually, the first step presupposes as a previous condition that there are at least n points with absolutely no links between them. Once laid out, these n points can be used to build the representation of the entire repertoire, simply by applying the rules of mapping which we have already studied.

The simplest figure necessary to support the repertoire will therefore be a completely nonconnected graph containing at least n points.

Naturally, we could trace any of the graphs in Figure 15 onto the com-

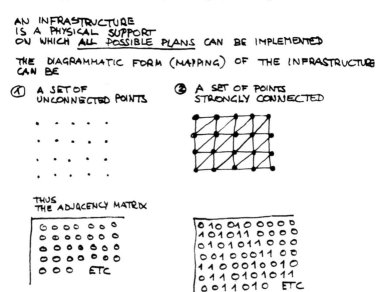

Figure 21

pletely nonconnected graph, simply by adding the connections between
certain points (or the sign 1 in the adjacency matrix for certain points).
The completely nonconnected graph, therefore, represents an *infrastructure* for the mapping of the complete list of possibilities (for example, the 24 million possibilities in Figure 17). This "abstract" infrastructure is truly the most indeterminate one possible.

So the entire infrastructure is represented by this set of unconnected
points. We can decode this abstract image by inverting the rules of mapping for connected graphs (which were: "a point represents an enclosure," "a line is an access," and "no room can be inaccessible"). De-
coded according to these rules, the set of unconnected points represents a set of inaccessible enclosures, as many as there are points.

When a future user makes a decision (a choice) the first question will
concern what connections to establish. They will be shown by a linkage
scheme for a certain number of points corresponding to the enclosures
he has decided to make accessible in a particular way. The linkage required by the client's choice will of necessity be included in the repertoire, and this choice made from the repertoire can be carried out in
the actual construction (the set of enclosures with no access) by creating the corresponding openings in the previously continuous walls.

In a technical rather than industrial context this is like an artificial
sort of troglodyte habitat, such as certain cultures have come to produce, in which the "envelope" of the enclosure is built first and then
doors and windows are "punched out."

Figures 22 and 23 show a model of this kind of infrastructure and its
corresponding mapping, along with several arbitrary examples of specific choices, represented in graphs and transposed onto an infrastructure.

This is only one example of an infrastructure effectively adapted to
a particular local industrial context. I have proposed this type of infrastructure to solve construction problems for low-cost housing in an
African nation. This proposition made it possible to combine mass production using local techniques with the very rich individual characteristics of a sophisticated culture.

Another way of transposing the principle of the graph of unconnected

THE „TROGLODYTE" INFRASTRUCTURE
CORRESPONDS
TO A SET OF UNCONNECTED POINTS

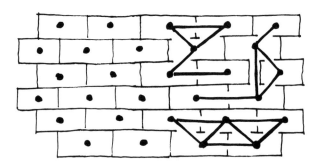

ITS PHYSICAL REPRESENTATION
IS A SET
OF UNCONNECTED ENCLOSURES

SEVERAL ARBITRARILY CHOSEN PLANS
(CORRESPONDING TO THE THICK LINE
GRAPHS) CARRIED OUT IN THE
INFRASTRUCTURE
BY OPENING PARTITIONS

Figure 22

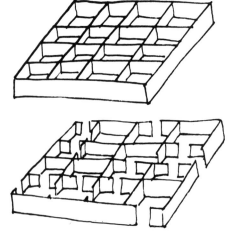

„TROGLODYTE"
INFRASTRUCTURE

ARBITRARILY CHOSEN
PLANS
CARRIED OUT
IN THE INFRASTRUCTURE

Figure 23

points into hardware is to use the complementary figure: that of a planar network having the maximum number of connections between points, so that all enclosures mapped by this figure would be as interconnected as possible from the start (thus having maximum accessibility). It would follow that all the points in the map of the infrastructure would be linked as often as possible in a planar graph or in a *planar network* (I have already spoken of saturated graphs in Section 3.2 and I shall deal with planar networks later on). A particular choice could be schematized by blocking out one or more of the links from the maximum number, which would correspond to building a wall in order to seal the access between certain enclosures, rather than punching out an opening, as in the first example. The kind of hardware that permits the use of this technique is called the "skeleton" type, shown in Figures 24 and 25.

The example in our illustration certainly displays a wealth of forms (since a large number of labels was included). It is easy to obtain so much variety within the infrastructure whether it is of the troglodyte type or the skeletal type, but I should add that it is easier from a technological point of view with the skeletal type.

3.5 A TECHNOLOGICAL NECESSITY: THE CHANCE TO MAKE MODIFICATIONS

Figure 6 in the first chapter showed how the future user made his decision—a process which eliminated the communication bottlenecks. The figure was made up of two loops: the first represented the act of choosing, the second represented transposing the decision into hardware. Now we are going to add a third loop—one for corrections—to the diagram (Figure 26).

The significance of the diagram is this: the future user chooses an initial arrangement of enclosures, which are built inside the infrastructure. After using it for a while, he discovers that he would like to change certain aspects of the arrangement, for reasons of his own (perhaps a change in his life style, a miscalculation, change in an exterior factor). He will make a second choice (with or without the repertoire this time) and will decide on a new arrangement for his enclosure.

A SKELETON INFRASTRUCTURE
CORRESPONDS TO A SET
OF STRONGLY CONNECTED POINTS

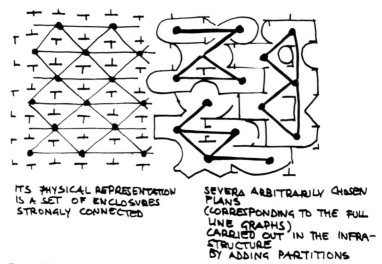

ITS PHYSICAL REPRESENTATION
IS A SET OF ENCLOSURES
STRONGLY CONNECTED

SEVERAL ARBITRARILY CHOSEN
PLANS
(CORRESPONDING TO THE FULL
LINE GRAPHS)
CARRIED OUT IN THE INFRA-
STRUCTURE
BY ADDING PARTITIONS

Figure 24

Naturally, his new choice will correspond to one of the possible solutions; it will therefore be capable of realization within the infrastructure, and the opportunity of implementing it will be his due. (I shall
deal with the technological conditions for carrying this out in Chapter
6.)

Now, although the point of the infrastructure was a solution which
we could achieve by abstract reasoning, and although the reasoning led
us to define the infrastructure as a type of "hardware," it is not the
same with modification, the necessary conditions for which cannot be
determined in this way.

Actually, the possibility of modification is not a problem of abstract
structure, like the repertoire and the infrastructure, but rather a simple
technological problem, at least in its principal aspects. However, we
can state in abstract form the conditions for making modifications by
saying: *"Everything within the infrastructure* (and therefore *the whole*

process of opening up or of shutting off rooms) *must be reversible."*
The hardware must be changeable—only the infrastructure can be rigid
and fixed in place. If I wanted to make a diagram that conveyed this
statement visually, I would draw only the infrastructure in ink and use
pencil for the connections and labels. Modification would consist of
rubbing out some of the lines with an eraser.

I think that in thus separating the infrastructure, which corresponds
to a set of unconnected points, or to a saturated graph, from its "filling-
in," which is the changeable hardware corresponding to lines and labels
that are added or removed, I have succeeded in articulating the fundamental conclusion of this chapter. I shall get to its technological aspect
in Chapter 6. Here we are interested only in the model.

3.6 KEEPING A HISTORY OF MODIFICATIONS
If it is possible to make modifications, then the forms of filling-in for
the infrastructure (for instance, opening or insertion of partitions) will
change with time.

All possible changes, along with all possible variations, will of course
remain in the complete list of possibilities (links and labels). It is inter-

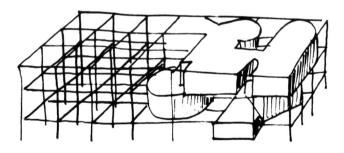

SKELETON INFRASTRUCTURE

EMPTY
INFRASTRUCTURE

SEVERAL ARBITRARILY CHOSEN
PLANS
CARRIED OUT IN THE INFRASTRUCTURE

Figure 25

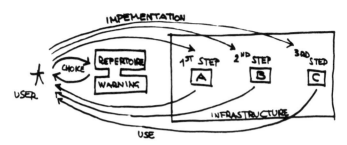

THE USER MODIFIES THE ARRANGEMENT CHOSEN AND
CARRIED OUT WITHIN THE INFRASTRUCTURE, EVEN AFTER
IT WAS CARRIED OUT. HE DOES IT IN ACCORDANCE WITH
THE WAY HE PREFERS TO USE IT IN THE FUTURE.
THE SEQUENCE ABC IS THE HISTORY OF HIS MODE OF USE.

A B C COULD MEAN, FOR EXAMPLE, ON THE BASIS OF THIS LIST

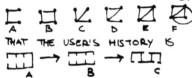

HIS HISTORY IS THUS REPRESENTED FROM THE COMPLETE LIST OF
SOLUTIONS, WHICH SERVES AS A REFERENCE LIST.

Figure 26

esting, and important, to be able to follow the history of these changes,
to note the sequence of different modifications that users make over a
particular span of time, transforming one linkage represented by the
graph G_n^x into another, represented by the graph G_n^y. If planning has the
least hope of becoming a scientific (or simply a conscious) activity, it
will fulfill it only by recording these "histories" and by trying to detect
the regularities which govern them. It will not be an easy job. We shall
study the tools for such research in Chapters 4 and 5.

For now, we shall think about the problem in its simplest form.

Let us imagine that in a given context a series of modifications have
been made within a particular infrastructure. And to simplify the example, let us suppose that only four elements (four kinds of filling-in)
were involved at each stage of the modifications. We shall use the complete list in Figure 26 as a reference, and in the same figure we shall
describe, step by step, the sequence of different arrangements of link-

ages that a fictitious observer would have seen.

For the "configurational history" of a particular user's four-room linkage, we shall use a sequence like *a d b b d e d*. We shall come back to this idea later on.

There is another history that the observer might see: a change not in the linkage, but in the use weights of the different enclosures. Figure 27 gives an imaginary example (taken, for purposes of demonstration, from the diagram in Figure 26).

When the use weights change, the local efforts change with them (*dw* being dependent on *w*), for each particular element of the linkage of enclosures.

We could describe this history in yet another way: first by drawing up a complete list of all the possible distributions of use weight (all the possible labels for a graph of *w*'s for a given graph), then by calculating local efforts for each distribution. I shall demonstrate this procedure using the same graph from Figure 27. Figure 27 shows a list of weight distributions for this graph, where the weights allowed for are $w_x = 1$ or 2.

This table constitutes a complete and well-ordered list for all the distributions of *w* that are possible in a graph of four points of the type in Figure 27, with densities of 1 or 2 (2 labels) and shows all the possible local efforts on the same graph. Once we have this table, we can use it to follow the history directly after observing the events (or use variations) in the corresponding linkage of enclosures for regular periods. For example, we might get Table 1.

Table 1

step	1	2	3	4	5	6 . . .
distribution	3	7	12	6	3	10 . . .
$\Sigma \Sigma$	19	24	29	29	19	24 . . .

In order to detect an eventual underlying regularity, it is important that the list of distributions be well ordered and drawn up according to a certain rule (such as a combinatorial operation).

THE GRAPH [A B C D graph] REPRESENTS THE PLAN [plan diagram B, A, C, D]

MR X GOES TO EACH ROOM ONCE OR TWICE A DAY.

THE COMPLETE LIST OF MODES OF USE FOR THIS APARTMENT OCCUPIED BY MR X WILL BE THE FOLLOWING:

(THE SIGN ● FOR A ROOM INDICATES THAT MR X GOES THERE TWICE A DAY).

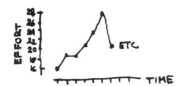

	I	II	III	IV	V	VI	VII	VIII	IX	X	XI	XII
W$_A$	1	1	2	1	2	2	1	2	2	2	1	2
W$_B$	1	2	1	1	2	1	1	2	1	1	2	2
W$_C$	1	1	1	2	1	2	2	2	2	2	2	2
W$_D$	1	1	1	1	1	2	2	1	1	2	2	2
$\sum w.d : E_A$	3	4	3	4	4	4	6	5	5	5	6	6
E$_B$	5	5	6	7	6	6	9	8	7	9	9	10
E$_C$	4	6	5	4	7	5	5	7	6	6	7	8
E$_D$	4	6	5	4	7	6	5	8	7	6	7	8
$\sum E$	16	21	19	19	24	21	24	28	25	26	29	32

A CASE HISTORY FOR MR X COULD BE THE SEQUENCE: I, IV, III, VI, II, V, VIII, VI. HIS EFFORT HISTORY WOULD BE: 16, 19, 19, 21, 21, 24, 28, 21, ETC

[graph: EFFORT (28, 26, 24, 22, 20, 15) vs TIME, with curve rising, labeled ETC]

Figure 27

3.7 AN APPLICATION OF THE REPERTOIRE: THE FLATWRITER

Thanks to a machine which I call the Flatwriter, each future inhabitant
of a city can imprint his personal preferences with respect to his apartment (flat) to be, using symbols which put in visual form the different
elements of his decision so that the builder as well as his neighbors can
understand what his choice is.

In other words, this machine contains a repertoire of several million
possible plans for apartments, knows how to work out instructions
about the characteristic consequences of the way each future inhabitant
would use an apartment, and finally, can determine whether or not the
site chosen by a future inhabitant will risk upsetting the other inhabitants.

Along with the Flatwriter I foresee the actual building of an infrastructure, of an empty, multileveled framework which contains a utilities network: water, gas, electricity, and sanitation.

The "organigram" (working plan) of the Flatwriter is shown in Figure
28.

Let us explain this working plan in terms of a certain Mr. Smith's
decisions, and see what answers and advice the machine would give.
STEP 1
Mr. Smith is presented with a keyboard. The keyboard contains
1. all of the connections and the configurations which three spaces
(just to keep the example simple) could have among them;
2. all the shapes which each space could have with regard to these connections (and in a technological context defined at the start);
3. all the positions which the kitchen and bathroom equipment could
occupy in a given space;
4. all the orientations the apartment could have.

Mr. Smith types on the keyboard just as he would type on a regular
typewriter. He chooses a configuration, than a shape for each room in
his apartment; he installs a kitchen and a bathroom, and finally he decides which direction his apartment will face. He has used eight or
nine keys, on a keyboard of fifty-three keys, to choose his apartment
out of the 24 million possibilities which the machine offers.

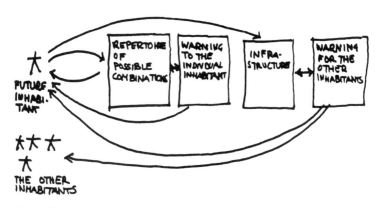

Figure 28

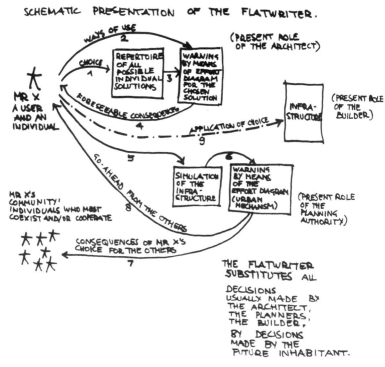

Figure 29

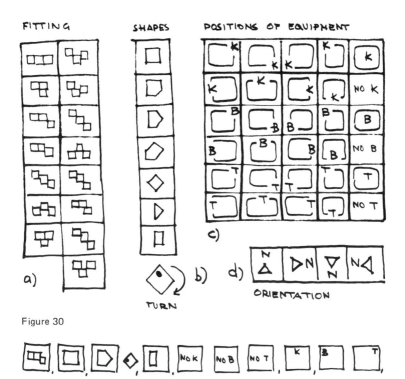

Figure 30

Figure 31

STEP 2

At this stage, Mr. Smith makes all the decisions and the machine simply prints them out, without contradiction or criticism. If, for example, Mr. Smith has touched the keys in Figure 31, the Flatwriter prints out the plan in Figure 32.

STEP 3

The Flatwriter prints out the cost of the apartment he has picked, calculating according to an appropriate classification for each item.

STEP 4

Mr. Smith moves on to another keyboard—the keyboard of weights. What it does is show him how many times a day he is in the habit of going into the first, second, and third rooms. One after the other, he touches the keys which represent how often he would come and go in the different rooms in the plan he has chosen.

STEP 5

Now the Flatwriter's first warning appears: it tells Mr. Smith the consequences of his choice, based on the plan and his way of life: the effort implied by his use of each room in his future home. If this effort, calculated from facts he has supplied, seems to be a disadvantage, Mr. Smith chooses another plan (perhaps by changing the distri-

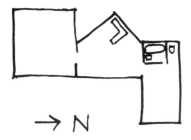

Figure 32

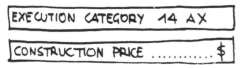

Figure 33

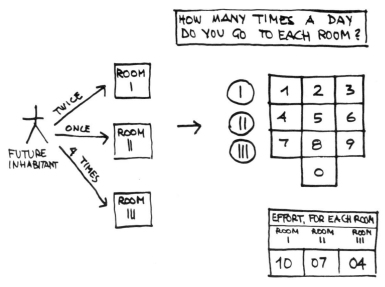

Figure 34

bution of functions for each room) or he may even think about changing his own way of using the rooms (the number of comings and
goings).

STEP 6

Next, the Flatwriter reproduces on a video screen a picture of the
plan of an infrastructure, an empty framework (Figure 35). Each empty
space in the framework has a number. When these spaces are taken up
by an aprtment, their outlines show on the screen.

I should mention that the infrastructure has been planned so that:
a. any choice can be realized in the empty spaces (voids);
b. any choice initially realized in these spaces can be changed and cor-
rected, without entailing any change in the infrastructure itself. All the
changes within the infrastructure involved only the movable parts (partitions, ceilings, floors) that have been inserted into the framework.

Mr. Smith types out the numbers of the spaces (voids in the infrastructure) where he wants to place the apartment he has chosen. He
choses the spaces in Figure 37.

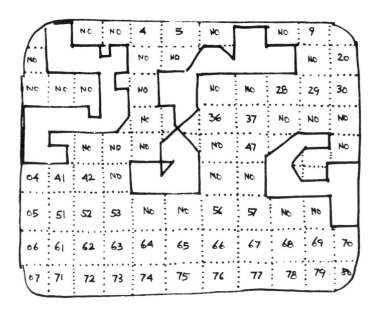

NO : UNDER CONSTRAINT
NUMBER : FREE

Figure 35

Figure 36

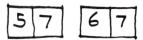

Figure 37

STEP 7
The Flatwriter inserts the outline of the apartment into the infrastructure, checking to see that the site Mr. Smith has picked out does not block the light, the air, or the access of one of the neighboring apartments that is already entered. In the case that his apartment should conflict with another one, the Flatwriter would answer:
Please Make Another Choice
STEP 8
Once the control mechanism has accepted the apartment Mr. Smith has chosen, on the site he would like, the Flatwriter recalculates the *effort diagram* for the entire infrastructure (efforts corresponding to all the apartments and public services already placed in the infrastructure). This diagram, in color, is displayed on the screen, superimposed on the infrastructure plan and the apartments already situated, or perhaps to the side on another screen.

The effort diagram informs the entire population of the infrastructure of changes implied by each new arrival for the utilization of the city or neighborhood (the infrastructure). To give a rough interpretation, the diagram shows whether the number of people passing by each dwelling has increased or diminished in comparison to neighboring dwellings. This information is very important: noise, quiet, commercial value, accessibility, and so forth are all included in the parameter *effort*.

CONCLUSION
The Flatwriter allows each future inhabitant of a city
a. to choose the plan and the characteristics of his apartment (his own individual environment), thus taking the place of the architect;
b. to choose the location of his environment in the city and receive an immediate "construction permit," thus taking the place of the planner and the city council;
c. to be informed of the particular consequences, directly concerning

him and his home, of each new choice or new decision being made throughout the city.

The Flatwriter thus puts a new informational process between the future user and the object he will use; it allows for almost limitless individual choice and an immediate opportunity to correct errors without the intervention of professional intermediaries.

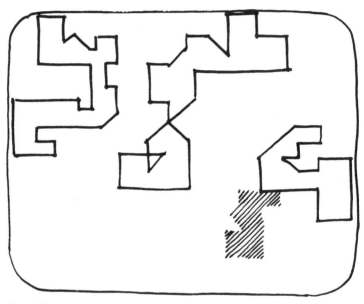

Figure 38

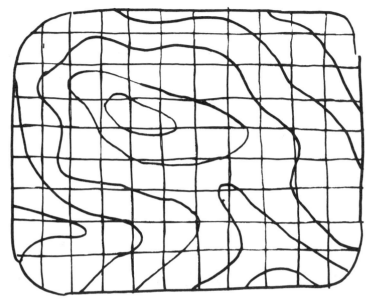

Figure 39

CHAPTER 4 URBAN MECHANISMS

4.1 COMPLETE PLANAR GRAPHS WITH $n \geqslant 7$: CROSSOVERS AND POTENTIAL CONFLICTS

In all the preceding sections, we referred to linkage schemes as the base for compiling a complete list of solutions to architects' and planners' problems. All other criteria were expressed by labeling (for example, shape, fixtures, use weight, and so forth). The linkage schemes were always presented in the form of convex planar graphs, and in all our examples, the number n of points in the graph (the number of enclosures) was very few.

We also talked about the impossibility of allowing crossovers in these graphs, because according to our rules of mapping they had no significance. Therefore, all the graphs which we studied were planar graphs.

I would like to come back to the idea of crossovers. Whatever system I propose to represent by graphs, its elements will always be symbolized by points, and the connections between the elements by lines. These points and lines can be marked with labels, which indicate some difference between two elements or between two connections. But what does it mean if crossovers appear within these graphs? They are points, but they do not represent what I have just referred to as elements of the system. They certainly do not represent connections. Consequently, we must either invent a new mapping rule to specify the exact significance of these points, or simply ignore them (which in itself would be a new mapping rule), and indicate that at such a point, lines pass over one another: in other words, that the graph is nonplanar. What, then, is the state of affairs that this new rule describes?

I wanted to show through this reasoning that a crossover represents a sort of uncertainty, as when a motorist comes to an intersection with no signs and does not know which road to take. A crossover implies some idea of danger, for there could be a collision, or simply a turn in the wrong direction, and there are no specific instructions that would eliminate the danger. What I am describing is a point of general uncertainty: where should he go? What may happen? And from what direction? I shall call the uncertainty represented by crossovers *potential conflict*.

While there may not actually be a conflict, in our example of the motorist, there is a good chance of one. However, the chances of conflict will be lessened if I receive adequate information about its proximity or if a regulatory device is installed at the crossover.

Earlier, this consideration led us to an interpretation of crossovers as full-status points, but representing special enclosures, such as stairs, corridors, and so on, which we can think of as regulatory devices.

But these crossovers are like rabbits (so are the conflicts, for that matter): they have a tendency to multiply at a terrifying rate. The number of crossovers in a complete graph (a graph where every point is joined to every other point) is a function of n (which represents the number of full-status points in the graph). The formula for finding the number (a conjecture of Mr. Anthony Hill's) has not yet been verified. It is

$$CKn = \begin{cases} 1/64 \ (n-1)^2 \ (n-3)^2 & \text{if } n \text{ is an uneven number} \\ 1/64 \ n(n-2)^2 \ (n-4) & \text{if } n \text{ is an even number.} \end{cases}$$

This means that the number of crossovers (and therefore of conflicts) increases proportionally as the fourth power of the number of points which are to be completely linked.

It also means that each time that there are more than seven points to connect, there will be more crossovers than linked points. Therefore, if we suppose that the crossovers represent stairs or corridors, a linkage of seven main enclosures would necessitate nine hallways or stairways, if every enclosure were to be connected directly to every other; and each hallway and staircase would have four doors (see Figure 40).

If we want to construct the most complete possible n graph with no crossovers, we will notice that instead of the $LK = n/2 \, (n-1)$ connec-

A GRAPH OF MORE THAN 7 POINTS, IF COMPLETE,
WILL HAVE MORE CROSSOVERS THAN POINTS (SUMMITS).

A LINKAGE OF MORE THAN 7 ENCLOSURES
WILL HAVE MORE CORRIDORS (OR STAIRWAYS) THAN ENCLOSURES.

THE COMPLETE GRAPH K_7
HAS 9 CROSSOVERS

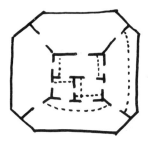

THE PLAN CORRESPONDING
TO K_7
HAS 9·2=7 CORRIDORS OR
STAIRWAYS

Figure 40

tions established in the complete graph, we can allow no more than $LS = 3(n-2)$. The number of connections missing with regard to the complete graph will be: $LM = 1/2\ (n^2 - 7n - 12)$.

It is clear than when n is a large number, LM becomes very large compared to LS. In other words, if we are to assemble a great many points (or enclosures) it is impossible to complete a perfectly connected organization.

4.2 NETWORKS

As I have already described, plotting a graph with a large number of points soon implies a large number of crossovers, sources of potential conflicts, and only some kind of regulatory system can reduce the chances of conflict.

Since there are many crossovers, there must also be many regulatory devices, which brings us to a most uneconomical situation. It would be more economical, for instance, to install a few complex regulators instead of many simple ones.

I have already proposed another way to make this system more economical, and that is to use saturated graphs, which have *LS* connections, instead of complete graphs with *LK* connections. This arrangement allows us to have *LM* pairs of points indirectly linked. We could present the same problem in still another way: as a set of *n* points. The complete list of possible connections (direct or indirect) will carry a number *LK*. If I plot all the connecting paths on a diagram of *LS* connections, the *LK* connections will all still be possible (let us call them itineraries instead of connections or paths). In this case, the same number *CK* of crossovers remains, but the actual crossing points will be regrouped on *n* sites. The number of regulatory devices could then be reduced by a power of four.

When an *n* graph with *LS* connections supports a complex system of itineraries, I will call this graph the *infrastructure of the system of itineraries* (by analogy to the infrastructure with the maximum number of connections, which I spoke about in Chapter 3). Figure 41 shows the saturated 6-graph used as the infrastructure of the complete 6-graph.

When there are a large number of points to be joined, the infrastructure becomes what is known as a network. In my terminology, a network is a graph which has a very large number of nodes. Here we will use exclusively planar networks. Actually, we can always draw nonplanar networks on a planar network by resorting to the appropriate system of labeling, which would show that there is a relation in space between one link and another, at a point of the planar graph. We can illustrate this process with the help of a photograph of a complex spatial structure. If it is a clear photograph, it is possible, at each point of the picture plane, to "read" which line passes in front of which, or which lines meet in a point. This photograph is an excellent example of a labeled network, where the clarity of the image at each point on the plane surface acts as a label.

The accuracy of this statement is easily demonstrated in Figure 40 by replacing the labels of an arbitrarily constructed network with overpasses and *underpasses* and *level crossings*. The labeled planar network which results constitutes an exact mapping of a nonplanar network.

In fact, the labeled planar network cannot be a picture of a spatial net-

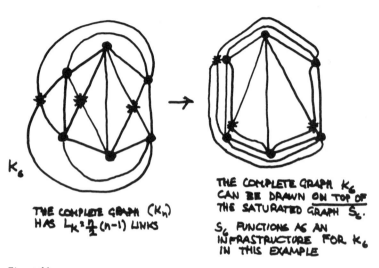

THE SATURATED GRAPH (S_H)
HAS $L_S = 3(n-2)$ LINKS

K_6

THE COMPLETE GRAPH (K_H)
HAS $L_K = \frac{n}{2}(n-1)$ LINKS

THE COMPLETE GRAPH K_6
CAN BE DRAWN ON TOP OF
THE SATURATED GRAPH S_6.

S_6 FUNCTIONS AS AN
INFRASTRUCTURE FOR K_6
IN THIS EXAMPLE

Figure 41

work unless it has at least two kinds of labels. If it has only one kind, it
can represent only a regular planar network or a set of lines bypassing
each other in space (Figure 43).

   Obviously, we can easily replace a network, planar or nonplanar, by
the corresponding adjacency matrix.

   Henceforth I shall use the term *network* to mean a graph with a large
number of points, where there are at least two different possible itineraries having no common point between any two points. These networks
will serve as infrastructure for a large number of itineraries and will
assure that the system works even if one of the itineraries is interfered
with, for the others will make the necessary connections possible. These
networks will be described by a diagram or a matrix, like the planar
graphs, but if necessary it will be possible to label them so that they
could be interpreted as nonplanar. They may be regular, and in this

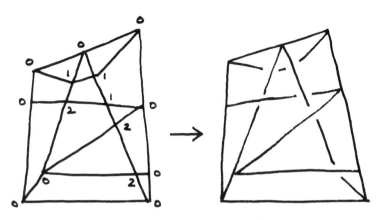

A LABELED PLANAR GRAPH (NETWORK)
CORRESPONDS EXACTLY TO A GRAPH IN SPACE

LEGEND: 0 : LEVEL CROSSING
           1 : ⊣⊢ OVERPASS
           2 : ⊥ UNDERPASS

Figure 42

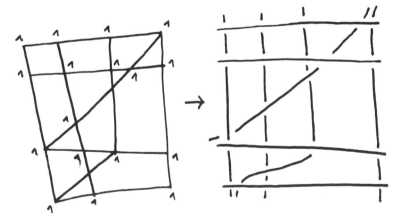

A PLANAR GRAPH
IS NOT A SPATIAL NETWORK'S MAP
UNLESS IT HAS AT LEAST 2 KINDS
OF LABELS

Figure 43

case, a rule describing the construction of the network in one area will be valid for the entire extent of the network.

The model for regular planar networks, which will be the focus of our attention from now on (since all other types of networks are derived from it) is the type called networks of homogeneous degree, that is, networks where the number of lines meeting at any one point is always the same. The *degree* of a point is the number of connections leading to or from it; consequently, in an adjacency matrix the degree of a point is given by the sum of all the values of its row.

There are four planar networks of homogeneous degree: those of degree (3), (4), (5), and (6). (I note the degree by putting the number that indicates it in parentheses).

These networks will be the general models which we will use to analyze systems composed of a great number of points.

4.3 EXAMPLE OF AN ANALYSIS USING NETWORKS: PATTERNS OF TRANSPORTATION

We have seen in Section 2.3 that before we analyze a system, we must first describe it using axioms (three, if possible). Once the description is complete, we assign a mapping rule to each axiom, and we compile a combinatorial list conforming to these rules. To each term on the list we attach a warning or a ranking on an arbitrary scale of values, or in accordance with arbitrarily established criteria. It should always be possible to express the corresponding warning numerically (for example, by the cost or local effort value, as in the case of the Flatwriter).

Let us try to demonstrate this method by applying it to the problem of transportation systems.

First, we look for three axioms, as in Section 2.3.

First axiom: a physical object moves on a line.

Second axiom: two physical objects can move along the same line only if they are going in the same direction.

Third axiom: two physical objects can move on two different lines on the condition that they do not arrive at the crossover of these lines at the same time.

First mapping rule: a transport system can be represented by a system of lines.

Second mapping rule: the lines of this system must carry only one arrow between two adjacent points.

Third mapping rule: all crossovers of the line system must be broken down into subcrossings of the different possible itineraries.

These mapping rules allow us to represent any transportation system by an appropriate network. These statements appear obvious (axiomatics always appear obvious) but they imply a very restrictive network selection: although the first rule allows us to use any network, the second requires that all the points in the network can be reached once the lines have been marked by arrows. Finally, the third rule shows each itinerary as an isolated component of the network (which leads us to the concept of the complete graph).

Within the restrictions imposed by the axiomatic description of a transportation system, certain requirements are not expressly stipulated, for example:

a. it is not stipulated that a moving object will necessarily touch all the points of the system in its path

b. it is not stipulated that a moving object must return to its point of departure.

We can add restrictions *a* and *b* to our axiomatics if it becomes necessary within a given technological context, but axioms are much more

THE 4 PLANAR NETWORKS OF HOMOGENEOUS DEGREE

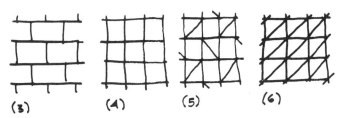

(3)   (4)   (5)   (6)

THE DEGREE OF A NODE INDICATES THE NUMBER OF LINES
LEAVING FROM AND ARRIVING AT THE NODE.

A NETWORK IS OF HOMOGENEOUS DEGREE
IF ALL ITS NODES HAVE THE SAME DEGREE.

Figure 44

general (weaker) than contextual statements.

The mapping which conforms to these three rules will include planar and nonplanar networks. Since the nonplanar networks are derived from planar networks by means of labeling, we will examine only the planar networks, reserving the designation *planar networks carrying more than one kind of label* for the nonplanar ones.

Since networks of homogeneous degree are the most suitable type for the study, we shall use them to map our axioms and then compare them to each other with reference to the specific problems that each axiom presents.

The first rule does not imply the selection of any one network over another, for all the networks are composed of lines.

The second rule determines how we place arrows on a network. Here we can add the "contextual" postulate (*a*) that reduces the number of moving objects, but each point of the network must still be accessible to at least one of the *axes* of movement.

The third rule concerns the nodes (the points) themselves, and examines the number of intersections clustered in one zone. All the itineraries that pass through a given point depend on the lines and arrows that meet at that point, and therefore on the degree of this point. So the decisive factor for this third rule will be the degree (sum of the values of one row in the adjacency matrix), broken down into groups of arrival arrows (entrance) and departure arrows (exit).

For a given network, the analysis will work this way: First step: plot arrows on the four homogeneous networks (of degrees 3, 4, 5, and 6) and in such a way that certain itineraries can traverse the network from one end to the other (axes) and that all the points can be reached by at least one of these itineraries. We will be able to establish a comparison, on the basis of the number of simple itineraries (or axes), for example, and on the basis of repeated use of certain parts of trajectories.

Second step: plot all the paths that pass through a given point of the network (we define as points of the network those of degree equal at least to 3), and count all the subintersections among these paths in the vicinity of the point.

Thus, we have compiled two complete lists (networks and paths), and

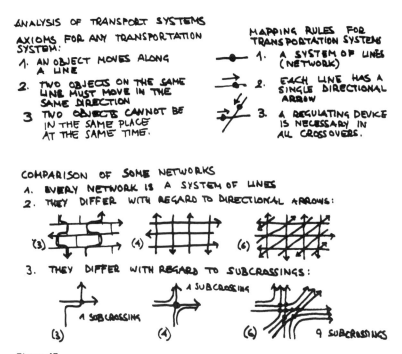

Figure 45

the two studies that we have made—of directional arrows and of sub-intersections—have given us numerical results which we can use as the basis for comparisons or as instructions. A network's properties of *direction* and of *intersection* do not represent values, advantages, or inconveniences, but they are in a sense intrinsic properties of the network. They will not be considered as advantages of inconveniences until they are introduced into a specific context that spells out the intensity, speed, dangers, and so on, of a particular transportation system. This implies likewise that a transportation system is not necessarily represented by the network itself (which has only the role of infrastructure), but that the system depends on how the infrastructure is used.

The result of this study of networks may lead us either to modify the context of transportation or the network. Either course of action may be applied by physical or nonphysical means (for example, by setting up a traffic code).

4.4 HOW DO YOU OBSERVE A CITY?

Let us broach another subject.

I would like to examine the way we observe a larger complex, such as a city, adhering to the postulates concerning objective descriptions which I established in Chapter 2.

To begin with, I must put forth the improbable hypothesis (so often unconsciously respected) that we are able to observe a city as if through the eye of God. In other words, we assume, in this case, that with some unknown instrument of observation we could see everything in this city, everything that happens in the streets, in the houses, in the heads of all the inhabitants, and of all the other living creatures, including dogs and microorganisms. Naturally, such vision is impossible.

Instead, we could consider using a television camera that films the city, night and day, from a helicopter. This camera would not see inside the heads of people or microoganisms, but it would record all the movements of all the people in the city. This record would show who went where, and when. But even if we could devise it, this instrument would be too costly to operate. In addition, we would need almost as many people to interpret the record as there were people living in the city. Therefore, instead of dealing with a city of 100,000 inhabitants *plus* 30,000 image decoders (a sort of secret police) we would actually be dealing with a city of 130,000 inhabitants *of which* 30,000 were policemen. Therefore, the tool of observation which would assure us of recognizing individual identities (*and* itineraries) would be inseparable from the city under observation; consequently, this tool would implicitly falsify (transform) the thing observed.

Thus, bit by bit, we have had to leave complexity out of our information because of practical problems: we abandoned all hope of recording the individual activities which are the origin of specific movements, and then had to forego knowing the identities of the people making these movements.

We could doubtless observe individual itineraries (without knowing

specific identities), but even that would be very expensive and very
complicated, given the state of our technology. But the outward life of
a city is nothing other than the individual movements of its inhabitants,
precipitated by their motivations. All that is essential to the life of a
city is thus impossible for us to observe on the basis of our present
knowledge.

Then what is the best way to observe life in a city, using the tools we
have?

If we cannot observe people's motivations, their identities, or even
their itineraries, we can at least count the number of people arriving at
a given destination, without worrying about knowing who they are,
their reasons for coming there, or the routes by which they came. This
is an observation—very limited in scope—which we can make, counting
mechanisms such as turnstiles and photoelectric cells having been in
use for some time.

Let us think of what constitutes "movement" in a city. I can count all

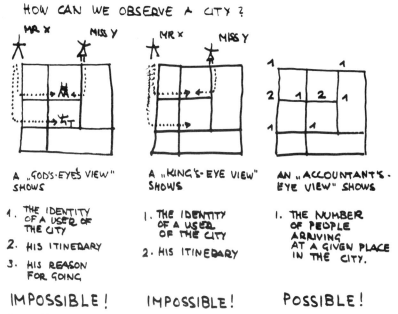

HOW CAN WE OBSERVE A CITY?

A "GOD'S-EYES VIEW" SHOWS

1. THE IDENTITY OF A USER OF THE CITY
2. HIS ITINERARY
3. HIS REASON FOR GOING

IMPOSSIBLE!

A "KING'S-EYE VIEW" SHOWS

1. THE IDENTITY OF A USER OF THE CITY
2. HIS ITINERARY

IMPOSSIBLE!

AN "ACCOUNTANT'S-EYE VIEW" SHOWS

1. THE NUMBER OF PEOPLE ARRIVING AT A GIVEN PLACE IN THE CITY.

POSSIBLE!

Figure 46

the people arriving at a given spot. But I shall never know why they are coming (motivation) or from where (names, addresses, preferred itineraries).

The only observations I can make about life in a city are thus
1. How many people arrive at a given spot and with what frequency
2. What constitutes the network for the transportation system that enables them to reach a particular spot.

This brings us to a schema for the city which lends itself to the kind of information we learned about in the preceding chapters: we will represent the city as a network (hence as a graph with a large number of points). In every sector of this network, we will note the number of people arriving during an arbitrary span of time.

4.5 THE URBAN MECHANISM

The picture in Figure 45 is a familiar one: it is a linkage scheme with labeling that describes use weight (see Section 3.3). This use weight has been calculated from the frequency of visits to an enclosure or to a given complex. In this sketch which shows the city, it represents the frequency of visits to an enclosure within a two-dimensional complex.

We have used use weight to calculate local effort, represented in the effort matrix by the sum of the values in each row. We can proceed in the same way here.

The local effort diagram noted on this plan can be interpreted in a very vivid way: The little person drawn on the diagram at point A lives at A. All week long he must make trips into town for work, social life, entertainment, shopping, and so forth. Even he does not know what trips he will make this week, this month, in the coming year. A new job, new friends, or the prospect of a bargain may take him to any part of the city. Getting from his home to any point in the city will involve a certain number of obstacles: distance, delays at intersections, detours around one-way streets. The more numerous the obstacles, the more effort he will have to expend to complete the trip.

Not knowing for sure where in the city Mr. A. has gone, we can work only on the basis of probabilities. Most likely, Mr. A. has gone to a place where many other prople have gone too. However, it is possible

FACTS WE CAN KNOW
ABOUT A CITY:

1. THE NETWORK OF PATHS
(INFRASTRUCTURE)

2. THE NUMBER OF PEOPLE
WHO HAVE ARRIVED
AT A GIVEN POINT
DURING A GIVEN PERIOD

THESE FACTS
ARE SYSTEMATIZED
IN THE "LOCAL EFFORT" MATRIX
ACCORDING TO THE FORMULA

$$E_A = \sum_{x=1}^{x=N} d_{Ax} \cdot W_x$$

THIS MATRIX CAN BE REPLACED
BY THE EFFORT DIAGRAM FOR THE
CITY, WHICH IS EASIER TO READ
THAN THE MATRIX.

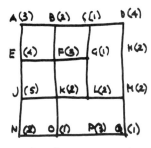

X(2) : ARRIVAL NUMBER
AT POINT X

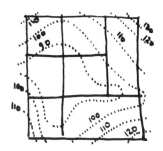

Figure 47

that Mr. A. did not go to this well-frequented spot. In that case, there
is a greater probability that Mr. B. went there. If Mr. A. and Mr. B.
have both gone elsewhere, then Mr. C.'s visit to that spot is even more
probable. And so forth. If there has been a crowd in one place, we are
sure to end up by finding someone who has been there!

This means that the number of arrivals (use weight) in one sector of
the network is proportional to the probability that any person chosen
at random in the city will in fact go to this sector. So we consider the
weight as proportional to this probability, and the distance (or time) as
proportional to the difficulty in getting to a given sector. Consequently,
we may say that the effort is proportional to the product of the difficulty in getting to a given point, multiplied by the probability that
someone will actually go to that point.

Thus, $E'_a = d_{ab} \cdot w_b$, assuming that there are only two points in the
entire town, a and b. (E'_a is the local effort required for a person's effective use of the city if he lives in a; d_{ab} represents the distance he must
travel and the difficulties he must surmount to get from a to b; w_b is

the number of people arriving at *b* in one week.

N. B. Naturally the time span can be of any length, and I have chosen a week only as an example. For practical purposes I could choose anything from a second (almost continuous calculation) to a year. In any case, if the calculated effort values are to be useful as a basis of comparison, we must define precisely the time span on which the calculation is based.

If our network includes *n* points, the local effort for point *a* will be given by the sum of all the effort necessary to get to any point in the network:

$$E_a = \sum_{x=1}^{x=n} d_{ax} \cdot w_x$$

Thus the diagrams of effort calculated in Figure 45, which show the relative ease with which a person living at a given point could adapt to some unforeseeable change in the way the city is used, in the course of his comings and goings. These figures have no absolute value; they are only parameters which enable us to know exactly which of two homes in the same city offers more advantages with regard to trips throughout the city, no matter how the inhabitant's situation may change.

To reintroduce an expression I have already used, the effort values serve as a *warning* to the user of any set of enclosures that is very complex and is used by many people.

In other words, this warning tells him about the mechanism of the city. And the effort parameter is thus a characteristic of the urban mechanism, which is composed, as are all mechanisms, of two elements: the infrastructure (the network) and its mode of use (probable choice of termini for itineraries expressed by the number of arrivals).

4.6 PROBABILITY AS A FREQUENCY CONCEPT OR AS A GAUGE

Again I must expand on a few thoughts of a theoretical nature relating to the concept of probability as it is used in my model of an urban mechanism.

Probability (which is not taken here in the sense of a mathematical

entity) is based on the calculation of the number of positive results
(successes) obtained in the course of a stated number of attempts (tests).
This calculation indicates the frequency of a particular event among a
limited number of events.

But another interpretation comes closer to my way of thinking. Let
us imagine a sequence of events. Given complete information on the
order in which they happen, I can always predict which events will
follow which (if, for example, there is a cause-and-effect relationship
among them). The probability that my prediction is accurate will have
a value of 1: my information is therefore good. On the other hand, if
my information about the order of events is poor, my predictions will
be much less sure than they were in the first case. Thus I will make my
predictions for a fixed number of test cases, and I will attribute a frequency probability to them (the number of correct predictions in relation to the total number of predictions made).

Now let us suppose that two people observe the same sequence of
events. One of them has good information and the other has poor information. The first person's predictions will have nothing to do with
probability, because a probability of 1 is equivalent to certainty.

The second person's predictions will be "reliable" to a degree expressed by the proportion of his correct predictions to the total number of predictions he makes. This is a frequency probability used as a
gauge of information.

But even if a third observer (I, for example) know the exact extent of
the second person's information, it will only allow me to count on a
certain degree of precision or error in his predictions, a degree proportional to the extent of his information. And even if the third observer
also knows the order of events with as much certainty as the first observer, it will not help him guess whether the second observer's next
prediction will be accurate or not.

The quality of the second observer's information will not depend absolutely on the original series of events but uniquely and exclusively on
his degree of knowledge.

In this sense the frequency probability is not a property of the events
whose frequency is the point of the calculation, but rather a property

of the information the observer possesses concerning those events, for it really represents the frequency of his accurate predictions. This scheme shows how we can use probability as a gauge of information. This probability will always be characteristic of the way a person has obtained his information (and, implicitly, it will also be characteristic of his means of observation).

In our urban mechanism model, the concept of probability will be used in this second sense: use weight is proportional to the probability that a person will go to a given spot (given the possibility—or the difficulty—of observing where he actually goes). This concept of probability allows us to gauge the quality of information furnished by the "tool" (counting) used to observe movements in the city.

Movements in a city are to some extent similar to the Brownian movement of particles in a liquid. This similarity does not derive from an analogy between the systems themselves, but from the way we obtain information about the two kinds of movement: in the case of Brownian movement, one can observe neither the "motivations" nor the "identities" of the molecules. The mathematical model that we use is like the one that describes Brownian movement. We call it a *model of probability potential.* Thus the effort map, which demonstrates the distribution of local effort values throughout the city, constitutes a map of *use potential,* describing the situations created by people about whose movements and behavior I can obtain only very poor information.

The mathematical model which describes the potential of any point in the city is actually a sum of products, in essence representing the results of operations of the "union of sets" type, the only kind of operation allowed in objective descriptions (see Section 2.2).

4.7 THE EFFORT MAP: ITS CHARACTERISTICS AND USE

The effort map is not merely a mathematical construction showing the characteristics of information obtained by an observer of the city. Its applications are very practical, for it communicates to us, in very simplified form, the facts necessary to make a decision, thus giving *all the users* of the city the chance to participate in this decision, in a manner consistent with the process of democratization which was my original premise.

Like all mathematical tools, this effort map "creates" information. It yields more facts than it was originally necessary to put into it to obtain this body of new information. This phenomenon is explained by the fact that data introduced into the map belong to two distinct and virtually unrelated sets: the physical network on the one hand and on the other our knowledge about behavioral characteristics expressed in numbers of arrivals (or weights). The map achieves a synthesis of these two sets by placing one in relation to the other, in the same way that the city itself constitutes a "real" synthesis of the corresponding "real" sets that are its components, its physical framework and the behavior of its inhabitants. Naturally, the physical framework is the least important of the two sets (the physical city, after all, is nothing but a ruin if it is not inhabited), but interventions (transformations) are easy to bring about in physical constructions and almost impossible in behavior because of the great inertia it displays.

The effort map derived from urban mechanisms represents a "multiple warning," based on the same principle as the local effort matrix, that I have established for simple configurations such as a linkage of spaces. The effort matrix has become a warning system that makes possible a simple numerical (therefore objective) comparison of the results of different uses of a single configuration, or from the identical use of different configurations. It plays the same role as the effort map, with two fundamental differences:

1. It involves a complex system of configurations (a network)
2. The chart keeps *all* the users of a complex (inhabitants) informed simultaneously.

Let us proceed to an imaginary application of this method, step by step:

The first question must deal with the meaning of the local effort value; it represents the essential characteristic of a given site (address) within the complex. Instead of describing a place of residence as "centrally located," "outlying," or "on a main thoroughfare" (concepts which have no significance unless they derive from experience, and consequently cannot be defined before the complex is actually built), we will use the new method, which allows us to build and rebuild (modify) the model instantaneously, by reference to the projected complex. Thanks to the simple numerical value that expresses effort we can immediately define the "effort situation" of an address as many times as necessary and constantly compare two addresses with respect to their effort situations, a comparison which would be impossible to make if geographic location were the only known fact.

The numerical data supplied by this model are more precise than any expressed in words and allow us to translate effort values into simple images that we can all understand. For example, if site A in a city has an effort value associated with a particular behavior of the inhabitants equal to 105, and if a nearby site B has an effort value of only 98, the situation can be explained to a layman in the following manner: there will be 105/98 times more people passing through B than through A. That might be worthwhile for a shopkeeper to know. Or again, it will be 98/105 times easier to go anywhere leaving from B than from A. That might be interesting for a doctor to know. Obviously, if it is in the shopkeeper's or doctor's interest to live in a place of small effort value, the same does not hold true for a scholar, a musician, or an invalid who needs to live in seclusion. He might prefer the A address with its higher effort value.

The choice between two possible sites with high or low effort value is a private decision, different for each individual.

Consequently, the second important fact to note about the effort map is that it establishes no preconceived scale of preferences. Every decision concerning preferences remains exclusively in the hands of the individual: the model does nothing but provide an objective basis for comparison, established from available information about the city or the complex.

The third characteristic of the map is tied in with the idea of comparison: if we follow the model, there can be no isolated act or intervention in a complex. Every decision—such as construction of a building, a change in business hours, the building of a new road—has an immediate effect on every point in the city. Every intervention of this type, therefore, can modify the effort situation of every inhabitant in the city. The map offers the opportunity to communicate these changes in effort value brought about by each isolated intervention to *all the inhabitants* of the city, *at the same time.* We saw an example of this kind of information feedback to everyone other than the client who was making the choice—in the case of the Flatwriter.

The effects of every individual decision should be transmitted to all the individuals making up a community—instantaneously, insofar as possible.

I think of the effort map as a sort of meteorological map that shows the fluctuations of the urban mechanism, and I think that it is as much a matter of public interest to everyone as is the weather report. All the applications cited here are based on this analogy with the weather map, from which the effort map differs only in that the city mechanism can be influenced by the acts and choices of the inhabitants (for example, by popular vote or by a change in individual or collective behavior), while the weather, at least so far, is not subject to human will.

Before studying a real application, I must make an important observation about urban mechanisms: this model shows us a relationship between use effort (a parameter) on one hand, and, on the other, a set of observable data: the physical layout of the city (the network), including the number of arrivals at all points of the network (use weight). The effort parameter is a sum of products, and consequently (as we have seen in Section 2.2) there is always a finite list of ways to arrive at a given sum and therefore at a given effort value. Thus any one situation on the effort map may be obtained in many different ways, and in a single network which corresponds to a single effort map, there can therefore by a number of distributions of use weights, all different. We will consider these distributions as equivalent, even though they are visually different.

Another observation, just as important: "weight" represents the number of inhabitants who arrive at a point; the reason for these arrivals does not matter. So there is no difference between a change in the number of arrivals brought about by some physical intervention (construction or demolition of a building) and a change due to nonphysical intervention (some sort of attraction or restriction); either factor can allow a larger or smaller number of people to get to a particular place. For example, doubling the hours a store stays open doubles its use weight as surely as if the owners doubled the size of the building (obviously a highly simplified example).

Thus a change in use weight can be brought about by nonphysical as well as physical intervention; and a city mechanism undergoes important variations each year. A city like Paris, for instance, has an entirely different mechanism during the tourist season than it has during the rest of the year (the locations of termini in the network and the number of arrivals at each of these sites changes completely, even if there is no physical intervention such as street repair).

Thus the model of the urban mechanism gives us information of vital concern to the inhabitant; thanks to it, he can monitor the intentions of the architect, the planner, or the politician.

Let us summarize the essential objectives of the effort map by stating a few of its basic principles:

1. Establish a parameter which expresses the intrinsic features of a real city (or of any way of using a network).

2. Find this parameter exclusively by means of objective observation treated in the only way allowable for objective descriptions.

3. Use the parameter as a basis for comparison between two different cities (or two organizations), thus making possible a conclusion as to whether the systems are equivalent.

4. Give the parameter a form that is easy to interpret (a map).

5. It should be possible to obtain the same configuration on the effort chart through a set of different interventions (physical constructions or intangibles such as a political decision).

6. Plan the map so it can provide information about the "use situation" of the city simultaneously to *all* the inhabitants.

4.8 A HISTORY DEPICTED BY URBAN MECHANISMS

I have defined history (in Section 3.6) as a sequence of events in chronological order. This definition does not imply that there must be regularity (periodicity) in history, and the sequence of events may well depend only on chance.

To find out whether a history has some regularity (whether it involves a structure) or whether it is completely subject to chance (in which case it could be defined as a history with a very specific type of structure) it is necessary to describe its chronological sequence by using the terms of a unique and observable parameter. For example, we can describe a city's history in economic terms, or outline it according to an individual's description of his personal impressions. The first will be the history of the city's economy; the second will be the history of the individual. History thus interpreted is the history of a parameter, that is, the sequence of variations of the parameter in chronological order.

If we are looking for an underlying regularity, we will begin our research by seeing whether or not the sequence of variations in chronological order has some sort of structure. We will call this structure, which is governed by the rule of sequential composition, a *law of nature.* If we cannot discover a law of nature in the sequence itself, we can always find a relationship between two histories that are distinct but dependent on the same chronology (time scale). In that case, the law of nature that we find does not refer only to the "elements" whose histories we have used to discover a relationship; the relationship itself creates a new parameter which may have its own history.

We cannot discover a "history" without making use of observation as long as its underlying law of nature has not been established, nor can we start with the hypothesis that such a law must exist. On the contrary, our initial hypothesis will be that every history may be the result of chance. But once a law has been found by observing history, and if we repeat this observation enough times, we no longer need to observe histories of this kind, since we can reconstruct them all using the law of nature that we have established. Everything that I have said about using a model therefore means trying to establish the existence of some underlying regularity by showing the relationship between the *observed* history of a given city and a history which can be *constructed,* that of the corresponding generalized model.

This is how I have interpreted urban mechanisms: the effort map is the model, and the complete list of all the possible states of this model can be constructed. The actual city constitutes a similar, though much

more complex, mechanism. Still, even admitting that complexity, as
soon as we have reduced the representation of the city to what we
know about it (Section 4.3) the actual city mechanism can be effectively described using the effort map.

Once we have constructed the complete list of all the possible states
of the model, we must make the list a carefully ordered sequence by
defining the operation which transforms one state of the mechanism
into another state as the law determining this order (Figure 27 and
Table 1).

In connection with this well-ordered list of all possible states of the
model (which in itself constitutes a constructed history), we can note
the observed history of the mechanism represented by the model, and
start looking for regularities in this observed history by taking the constructed history as the *field* of variants in the observed history. (In the
example in Figure 27 there is a symmetry in line $\sum E$, for the five first
terms, and the differences $\sum E_n - \sum E_{n-1} - 1$ are 5, 5, -5, 5, and so
on, which shows a certain type of regularity. Of course, there can be
other types of regularity, and one would have to compare a great number of sequences to find them.

The principal steps that interest us are these:

1. To construct all possible states of the mechanism model.

2. To code, for the list, all these possible states.

3. To observe, over a particular span of time, different states of the
real mechanism (the city), presented in chronological order.

4. To record this history using the terms of the code established for the
list of possible states of this model.

5. To observe regularities in the "real" history as mapped on the "constructed" history (the list of all possible states of the model).

The "real" application of these operations can be depicted by an example: let us suppose that the number of arrivals (weights) in an existing city has three different brackets (1, 2, 3). For purposes of simplification, the city's capacity would be measured according to these brackets; each bracket would represent its number multiplied by ten thousand. Thus, bracket 1 signifies ten thousand, bracket 2, twenty thousand, and bracket 3, thirty thousand inhabitants arriving at a given

point in the city during a certain time span. If the total of the brackets
is 36 (in that case the city has a population of 360,000), for twelve
principle arrival points (numbered one through twelve), the distribution of weight in the city forms a finite list whose terms are

D_1: 1_1 1_2 1_3 1_4 1_5 1_6 1_7 1_8 1_9 1_{10} 1_{11} 1_{12} (10,000 arrivals at all points
in the city),

D_2: 2_1 1_2 1_3 1_4 1_5 1_6 1_7 1_8 1_9 1_{10} 1_{11} 1_{12} (10,000 arrivals at all points
from 2 to 12; 20,000 arrivals at point 1 only), and so on to

D_{26244}: 3_1 3_2 3_3 3_4 3_5 3_6 3_7 3_8 3_9 3_{10} 3_{11} 3_{12}.

This list of all possible weight distributions for this case (the list of all
possible states of the urban mechanism, necessarily containing all the
changes that can be effected by all conceivable physical and nonphysical interventions) determines the "field" of states of the mechanism.
Every conceivable event in its "history" that has some repercussion for
the mechanism (an epidemic, demographic shifts, a boom in tourism,
economic depression, reduction in working hours, introduction of cul-
tural attractions) is under some code number D_x in the complete list.
Everything, absolutely everything in this city of 360,000 inhabitants
and 12 districts (except the death of a large part of the population,
which cannot be recorded since there is no bracket of zero value), is
indexed under some term in this list of 26,244 terms, each representing
a well-defined state of the mechanism. This is a list of very modest size
for a computer.

Naturally, during any real time period, only a part of the complete list
of possible historical events will show up as real history. Since the
urban mechanism method uses only directly observable data (networks
and arrivals), the observer can note in chronological order all events he
has observed and then interpreted according to these data, and each of
the events will have its corresponding term in the list. This is how a
"real history" can be represented within the field of the model list.

History thus interpreted in terms of variations in local effort ($\sum d \cdot w$)
or global effort ($\sum E$ or $\sum \sum dw$) will express "tendencies" such as
a tendency for effort to increase or decrease or to fluctuate according
to a certain rhythm, or to approach some constant value, and so on.

Whether or not a tendency is desirable is, once again, a matter to be

decided privately by each inhabitant (he may express his opinion by
popular vote, for example); moreover, he can delegate this power to
elected or appointed representatives (which is done today). As soon as
all the inhabitants accept a tendency as desirable (for example, value
24 in the table preceding Figure 27), it is easy to determine which states
of the mechanism (thus which distributions of weight) can produce a
tendency that approximates the desired value. There will almost always
be more than one distribution of weight which will give the same value,
and consequently more than one way of obtaining it (in Figure 27,
steps 5, 7, and 11 all lead to a global effort of 24). Generally one of
these ways is easier to implement than the others, and the political
decision always lies in choosing this way. The political decision which
settles the question can be made by vote, on the condition that all
those concerned are aware of all the possibilities and their foreseeable
consequences. This information about the results of planning policies
(warning) is made possible by the model I have described.

4.9 THE UNPREDICTABILITY OF HISTORY

In the preceding section, I introduced the hypothesis that the history
of an organization—the history of a city, for example—could be a sequence of chance events. Before arriving at this statement, we had discovered that probability could be interpreted as a gauge of information;
thus absolute chance (the vaguest probability) is equivalent to the
lowest degree of information (absolute uncertainty).

As I have previously defined it, a law of nature implies the possibility
of reconstructing the next state of a mechanism from a given state of
this same mechanism, assuming sufficient reliability of observation.
Chance, on the other hand, implies that such an operation is impossible
and that a given state of the mechanism can be followed by any other
possible state.

But even this principle of uncertainty, or chance, is based on regularities
such as laws, structures an abreviation system, since it states that there is a
mechanism, that is, a system (of haphazardly assembled elements) capable
of passing through a finite number of possible states. (I have excluded infinity from our study as impossible on a practical level; see Section 2.2).

My whole method is based on the hypothesis that every organization in some way constitutes a mechanism, and that we can discover the method of observation that suits each mechanism, whatever it may be.

The present impossibility of predicting how this type of mechanism will function is the result of a long history of treating these problems in a nonscientific manner: it was "intuitive" observation (which claimed to observe what is unobservable because uncommunicated and uncommunicable, like personal motivations or individual values); it was making the assumption that a mechanism could pass through an infinite number of states (mistakenly ignoring the fact that it is impossible to construct an infinite number); and "intuitive" parameters ("good," "bad")—all these, which, disguising the personal values of the observer, got us to the state where prediction is impossible. An unforeseeable event is unforeseeable only before it happens; once it has occurred, it seems that it could always have been predicted. In fact a rough prediction would be quite possible if only we limited ourselves to less ambitious predictions (which would not attempt to give a detailed picture) and more objective ones (made always in reference to a complete list of possibilities). In this chapter my goal is to arrive at a better way to handle knowledge and foresight about organizations, especially cities.

If unpredictability is in practice only the result of a nonscientific approach to knowledge, and if improving this approach can give us accurate predictions, then once we have made these predictions, we must apply them. Now, a prediction put to use becomes a means of influence; those who have the advantage of accurate predictions are more powerful than those who do not. That is why, throughout the history of mankind, we find the will to keep knowledge secret, for the exclusive use of a ruling class (priesthood).

Today, we are rapidly breaking away from this "segregation" of information; but different pressure groups still try to maintain information scarcity in all the professional fields.

4.10 APPLYING THE METHOD OF URBAN MECHANISMS
The potential application of this method has two motives. The first is

the trend toward democratization, of which I have spoken at some
length, and the second is the attempt to arrive at a simple and strategic
way of predicting what will happen in a city.

Of the two, the most important use of the method lies in the struggle
for democratization, quite similar in application to the process I described in Chapter 3 for the Flatwriter. It seeks a solution to the problem of how to arrive at a group decision, or at group control, when all
inhabitants belong to the group making the decision but act as individuals, both in creating situations and in making decisions about them.
This schema can be summarized in a few words: the individual behavior
of each inhabitant produces a new state in the mechanism; its characteristics are fed back to him very rapidly (in real time), allowing the
inhabitant to modify his behavior if he is led to make a different decision on the basis of this feedback.

Let us assume that an individual or a specific group proposes some
actual intervention in the city (for example, the physical construction
of a new point of attraction or a legislative change such as an extension
of working hours). The new intervention is easily expressed as a new
use weight at one or more spots in the city (the number of arrivals
caused by the new intervention). The algorithm used to calculate all
the new effort values (local or global) is expressed by sums of products
obtained by adding the products of the distance covered times the
weights for all points so that no local effort value is unchanged even if
only one weight has been modified.

Local effort values (parameters that change with variation in weights,
or in itineraries) have no absolute significance. Their role is to be useful
in comparing two states of a single mechanism or of two different
mechanisms. So the only decisive factors are the differences between
local efforts referring to a single point. For example, if before intervention two blocks of houses, A and B, had a difference of effort values
$E_A - E_B = 105 - 100 = 5$, this meant that block A had a situation that
was 5 percent better than that of block B, with respect to use efficiency
for a person living in either one of the two blocks. If, after intervention,
the difference between the two local effort values has gone to 3, then
this means that A's condition has deteriorated or that B's has improved

by a value of 2.

Now every proposed intervention can be evaluated in this way, for each block of houses in the city, by reading this intervention as variations in local effort. Naturally, these variations will be different for each block, for the effort map does not necessarily change into one that is isomorphic to it. As we have seen in Section 4.6, these variations can be interpreted in layman's terms, such as the number of people passing by a given block of houses (sector of the network) within the city, or the accessibility of this block. Effort values are proportional to effective commercial values or to land values, or to nuisance factors such as congestion and street noise. If inhabitants throughout the city can learn, through variations in the parameter of local effort (by which they will recognize fluctuations in commercial value and any foreseeable disturbances), about the consequences of an intervention for the sectors in which they live, and thus for their own blocks, then they can take a position supporting or opposing the proposed intervention, according to their personal interests.

Thus we might imagine the "intervention permit" (like a regulation governing working hours or a construction permit) put to a popular vote whenever the proposed intervention was thought to bring about, or would bring about, significant changes (changes can be defined numerically according to the number of people involved). This vote could accept or reject the proposed intervention, or it could impose penalties proportional to the damages and inconveniences incurred by the community, as well as by individuals. (This is the function of warning the community that I described in the case of the Flatwriter.)

The ballot would be different for each block of houses (since the variation in the effort value would be different in each block, even if it were brought about by a single intervention.) This ballot could contain the list of all the alternative weights or situations the proposed intervention would produce. And, for each alternative, it would note the effort variation brought about in each block of houses. All the inhabitants would have the right to vote for one or more solutions, whatever they thought would give them the most favorable effort situations for their particular cases. Thus they would act according to their personal

EXAMPLE OF A REFERENDUM
ABOUT THE CITY

AN INTERVENTION WITH WEIGHT
W_x MAY HAPPEN ON ALTERNATIVE
SITES 1, 2, 3 AND 4.

FOR EACH HOME ADDRESS A
THROUGH P THE BALLOT
SHOWS THE CONSEQUENCES
(EXPRESSED AS „EFFORT")
OF EACH ALTERNATIVE.

HOME ADDRESS	A	B	C	etc
0	0	0	0	etc
1	+1	+1	0	
2	-1	0	+1	
3	0	+1	+1	
4	-1	0	-1	etc

(ALTERNATIVES)

THE VALUES OF THE ALTERATIONS
IN THIS EXAMPLE
ARE EXPRESSED AS „ATTRACTION"
$AT_{A4} = E_{A4} - E_{A,0}$

GIVING THE NUMBER OF PEOPLE
WHO WILL PASS BY ADDRESS A IF
THE INTERVENTION IS CARRIED
OUT ON SITE 4.

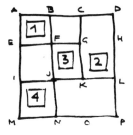

MR X, A SHOP KEEPER, WANTS CLIENTS.
HE HAS HIS SHOP IN A, AND HE WILL
THEREFORE VOTE, IN ORDER OF PRE-
FERENCE, FOR ALTERNATIVE 1,
THEN ALTERNATIVE 0 OR 3.

MR Y, AN INVALID, LIVING IN A, WANTS
LESS NOISE. HE WILL VOTE FOR
ALTERNATIVES 2 OR 4, BUT HE CAN
ACCEPT 0 OR 3 AS WELL.

Figure 48

preferences, but after having been properly informed of all the possible
consequences. Instead of being determined by a simple majority, an
evaluation of the results would choose the intervention that injured the
smallest number of people or that improved the situation of the largest
number of people.

This is one of the aspects of urban democratization.

Parallel to the actual vote, which involves calculating weights on the
basis of a rather long reference period (number of weekly, monthly,
or even annual arrivals) there is another, more up-to-date technique
that is based on continuous counting. Arrivals are counted around the
clock, and each arrival at each spot is immediately transmitted to a central computer which just as quickly calculates a readjusted effort map
of the city. The effort values calculated can be transmitted instantaneously to any point in the city, for example by means of municipal
machinery which I will call *city barometers.* At every street corner,
such a device would show the effort fluctuations at that spot at that
precise moment, something like the clock-thermometers that you see

on billboards. People would become as accustomed to checking for effort fluctuations in their cities as they are to checking the weather.

Providing the user with instantaneous feedback on fluctuations in the city has another consequence: if a user of the city can immediately find out the probable result of something he plans to do (take a certain road, stop at a certain place) then he can modify his initial intention if he wants to, after he learns about current fluctuations (a traffic jam in that direction, for example).

The implication of this is that the mechanism is self-adjusting and may tend toward a stable state. But that is only a hypothesis. In any case, once the information is sent back to the user, the mechanism will be different from what it was initially. If we could confirm the hypothesis that the mechanism tends toward a stable state (we would then have a Markovian process) it would probably be the most important contemporary discovery in the fields of architecture and planning, but we cannot establish its validity without a real experiment. I am less interested in defending this hypothesis than I am in suggesting the set of tools we would need for the experiment.

Another application which promises to be of scientific interest (as well as of practical value) is the use of signals for urban traffic. These signals, which would show each person his chances of continuing on his way by his chosen itinerary, would be installed far enough away from detour points so that he would have sufficient time to make a decision. A simple color code, for example, would show traffic jams on all segments of the road leaving from a specific detour point. Naturally, even one car setting out on a segment would immediately change this rate, and the next driver to come along would find a different distribution of expectation rates on the signal. Having been warned, some drivers would stick to their original routes, but others would change their minds. The functioning of these signals would depend on the same central effort map that we used in the preceding example, and each driver's decision would influence the central effort map by modifying the traffic.

There is a temptation to see this fluctuating readjustment as a process where game theory could easily be applied. Personally, I do not think that game theory can be applied to either planning or automobile traffic. For a game to be considered mathematical, there must be strictly established rules. There is nothing like that in the process of using a city, probably because we can obtain only very poor information about the individual, his motivations, and his behavior. Taking the process as a whole, there are neither winners nor losers in the use of a city. There is no game of competition, no exclusion of opponents from a "territory," and "individual strategies" do not affect the use of the city but in general more limited personal objectives; and whatever the objectives of a real, live user of the city, only he can know them in any matter that concerns him.

Thus, the implementation of the urban mechanisms model provides the user with immediate information about himself and other users. He must make his own decisions, then and there, and not depend on the advice of a planner. This is useful information, obviously, since it helps us to understand what is really happening in a city.

CHAPTER 5 GENERAL APPLICATIONS OF THE METHOD

5.1 LOOKING FOR LAWS OF NATURE IN HISTORIES

At the beginning of this book, we stated the principle that a science should be compelled to use abbreviations that everyone can understand. Obviously, these abbreviations can be used only in systems where certain repetitions are apparent (repetitions of elements, of operations, and so on). These repetitions allow for the elaboration of rules: we can call them rules (regularities) as well as "laws of nature," but they are not necessarily the properties of the thing observed (of nature); in fact, they are chiefly characteristic of the observer.

We also noted, in the preceding chapters, that the profession of architect or city planner, as presently practiced, is absolutely nonscientific; it recognizes mere rules of thumb, instead of demanding rigorous regularities. We have seen that this is a grievous state of affairs, for the new task that has fallen to this profession requires that it become scientific.

The question that we shall ask ourselves in this chapter is: how may potential regularities be discovered?

At present, other sciences, such as physics and biology, proceed by experiment in order to discover regularities. Experimentation means (as we saw in Chapter 2) the "repeatable" carrying out of a strictly defined sequence of operations; anyone must be able to perform it, and as often as desired; moreover, it must lead to the same result with each repetition; if not, we must conclude that the operational sequence is wrongly described, or else that it has been applied incorrectly.

In order to establish the "validity" of experiments in general, they must be repeated a great number of times and, if possible, with variations within the operational sequence. Therefore, it is difficult to apply experimentation to disciplines where processes unfold slowly, at great cost and risk, or even where the conditions prescribed by the operational sequence cannot be created at will. Now the process of constructing a building or a city is both long and costly, and therefore the series of necessary experiments cannot be easily performed.

In similar cases, we have to use "models" or "imaginary" experiments. The models are representations (mappings, with one-to-one relationships)* of a reality, reproducing all the properties that have significance for the observer. The model that we shall use to detect "laws of nature" in architecture and city planning will be the one we used in the preceding chapters (on models of urban mechanisms).

How would we conduct experiments with these models? We repeat the operations upon them as often as we wish, each time introducing one or several supplementary operations into the original sequence, and observing the changes that this produces in the results. Each of these experiments (carried out on models or even in some other way) represents an element of a "history," and a series of consecutive experiments represents the "history" itself.

The exhaustive (complete) list of *all* possible results (states of the model) constitutes the "field" of *all* the histories that may be produced for a given mechanism (a model or a real mechanism). The "real histories" observed can thus be represented by "constructed histories" (the histories of the model), within the "field" of all possible histories. If this field itself is constructed in a strictly ordered way, a history, or set of histories, may present its own regularities (which can be mathematically formulated) within the field. (As we have seen, chance itself constitutes a regularity: it deals with an *absence* of relations among any three arbitrarily chosen events *A, B,* and *C*; that is, the characteristics which differentiate a pair formed by two of these events cannot be found in the two other pairs that can be formed from the three elements. If, then, *AB, BC* and *AC* have no common characteristics, sets

*"One to one relationship" means that to each term of a set there corresponds a well-defined term in the map of that set, and that to every element in the map there also corresponds a well-defined element in the original set.

A, *B* and *C* constitute a fortuitous grouping (one due to chance.)

In order to detect regularities in this manner, I propose to follow the following five stages:

1. Construction of the field of reference
2. Actual observation of a group of histories
3. 'Mapping' the observed histories within the field of reference
4. Establishing the common characteristics of the histories represented
5. "Decoding" the observed regularities, by transposing them from represented histories into histories that can be observed in actuality: these regularities are the laws of nature that we are looking for.

I am going to follow this program in the following sections.

5.2 CONSTRUCTING THE FIELD OF REFERENCE: TYPES OF HUMAN BEHAVIOR BASED ON ABSTRACT CATEGORIES

Let us imagine that I wish to describe human behavior with the help of a complete list. To do this, I shall assume that certain categories of activities exist, whatever their nature (at the present time, architects use—with the cooperation of sociologists—categories of "work," "leisure," and "supply"). The individual behavior of any particular person can be described when we succeed in finding how often he performs activities belonging to one or the other of these categories, expressed, for example, by the fact of his "going to such a place" or devoting "so much time" to that activity; we thus establish the *frequency* of an activity during a given time of reference. I could, for example, describe my own type of behavior in the form of W:6, L:7, S:2 and that of my wife in the form of W:5, L:7, S:1, and so on.

Naturally, we could construct a finite list, comprising all the types of possible behavior, established according to these three categories of arbitrarily chosen activities. The type of behavior that would begin the list would take the form 0-0-0, describing the behavior of a person having absolutely no activity whatsoever (an invalid, for example), and the last term of the list would be behavior 7-7-7 (that of a hyperactive person), taking a week as the time of reference, and counting activities by simply noting whether or not they have been pursued on a given day, without mentioning the number of times they have occurred on that day.

This complete list of types of behavior, constructed from the hypotheses mentioned (8 frequencies and 3 categories of activities) would comprise $8^3 = 512$ different terms, based on the model:

	W	L	S
B_1	0	0	0
B_2	0	0	1
B_3	0	1	0
B_4	1	0	0
	. . . .
	. . . .
B_{512}	7	7	7

This combinatorial list contains any possible type of individual behavior, in the case of a description based on the categories "work," "leisure," and "supply," and for a weekly frequency of activity.

Of course, these categories were chosen rather hastily, and I am using them only because they are familiar. But one might very well choose them on any distinctive criterion, as, for example, "variations in blood pressure." One would then have category A, activities having no influence on blood pressure; category B, activities lowering blood pressure; and category C, activities increasing it. A list composed as a function of these categories A, B, and C would be complete when it appeared in the same exact form as the preceding one, and there would be no activity pattern imaginable that could not be found somewhere on the list, since all activity belongs to one of the categories, A, B, or C, and can be carried out with different weekly frequencies, just as in the preceding list. Thus these two lists equally well represent all possible types of behavior, provided that the number of frequencies and categories is the same, although they are based on different categories and both include 512 numerical expressions, which are exactly the same in both lists, and noted in the same order.

We would be able to construct such a list on the basis of any other imaginable categories, and naturally, the list would always be the same. The difference between these lists would lie in the fact that the

LET A, B AND C BE OBSERVABLE CATEGORIES OF ACTIVITIES, IN WHICH

A CAN BE "WORK", OR "SOMETHING THAT INCREASES BLOOD PRESSURE"
B   "   "   "BUYING", OR "SOMETHING REDUCING BLOOD PRESSURE"
C   "   "   "LEISURE", OR "SOMETHING HOLDING BLOOD PRESSURE STEADY".

WHATEVER MEANING IS ASSIGNED TO CATEGORIES A, B AND C, EVERY IMAGINABLE TYPE OF BEHAVIOR WILL BE INCLUDED IN THE COMBINATORIAL LIST BELOW.

THIS LIST SHOWS, FOR EACH BEHAVIOR TYPE, HOW OFTEN ACTIVITY A, B OR C IS PERFORMED DURING A REFERENCE PERIODE.

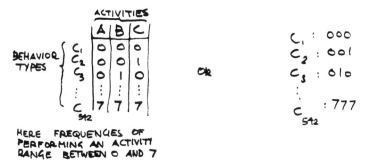

HERE FREQUENCIES OF PERFORMING AN ACTIVITY RANGE BETWEEN 0 AND 7

Figure 49

actual observation and the "proportion of occurrence" of each of the types of behavior would vary according to the categories chosen.

We shall call this list of 512 terms, each containing three symbols chosen from among the figures 0 to 7, a complete list of types of behavior based on three abstract categories of activities: in other words, such a list can very well constitute the "field" of any coherently observed "history."

If types of individual behavior expressed as a function of three abstract categories, and observed according to their weekly frequency, involve constructing a complete list of 512 terms, we must make a far greater list when dealing with collective behavior. Let us consider three abstract categories, 1, 2, and 3, making up a similar list; if, within a community, we decide to consider three fractions as significant, each comprising a third of the total population of that community, we shall have, as a complete list of the types of collective behavior, a list established according to the weekly frequency with which the abstract activities 1, 2, and 3 are carried out:

Categories of Activity			
	1	2	3
B_1	0	0	0
B_2	0	0	1
B_3	0	1	0
. . . .			
. . . .			
B_{512}	7	7	7
Types of individual behavior			

Fractions of the Population			
	1/3	1/3	1/3
B_1	000	000	000
B_2	000	000	001
B_3	000	000	010
. . . .			
B_{512}	000	000	777
B_{513}	000	001	000
. . . .			
$B_{158337880}$	777	777	777
Types of collective behavior			

In fact, these types of collective behavior would give us an enormous list, but one which we could maintain within the limits of a computer's capacity by a judicious choice of the number of categories of activities, of maximal frequency in the time of reference, and of significant fractions. Thus, we could construct the list of all possible collective activities, with reference to abstract categories of activities.

Aside from the fact that it is complete, this list is also well ordered, since its rules of composition (combinatorial) permit the determination, for each term on the list, of the one to follow. The list is thus well constructed according to the rules.

5.3 CONSTRUCTING THE FIELD OF DISTRIBUTIONS IN SPACE (CONFIGURATIONS)

Next, for the experimentation that is the subject of this chapter, we need a second list of *all* the possible physical distributions of theaters of activity, within *all* the possible networks of n points, and therefore, to use the terminology of the preceding chapter, the list of all possible mechanisms.

How shall we construct this list? First of all, we know from the preceding chapters that any given network of n points can be represented (mapped) by a binary sequence of $\frac{n}{2}(n-1)$ signs (see Section 2.5).

Consequently, in constructing a combinatorial list of all sequences of
this type (with the exception of isomorphic sequences), we shall obtain the combinatorial list of all networks of n points. This list will
have at most $2^{n/2 (n-1)}$ terms.

Moreover, we saw earlier (Section 3.3) that "use weights" could be
included in such sequences (representing a linkage scheme and therefore a network) in the form of "labels" placed, for example, above
each section representing a given point in the linkage. This means that
we can increase the list of binary combinations and insert into each
binary expression (and thus into each linkage scheme) all the "weight
distributions" (and therefore all the labelings) possible in a given network. If, therefore, for the sake of convenience, we consider k "degrees of weight" (w_x having the value $1, 2, 3 \ldots k$) to be significant,
then the possible weight distributions in the network of n points cannot exceed the value: $C = 2^{n/2 (n-1)} \cdot k^n$.

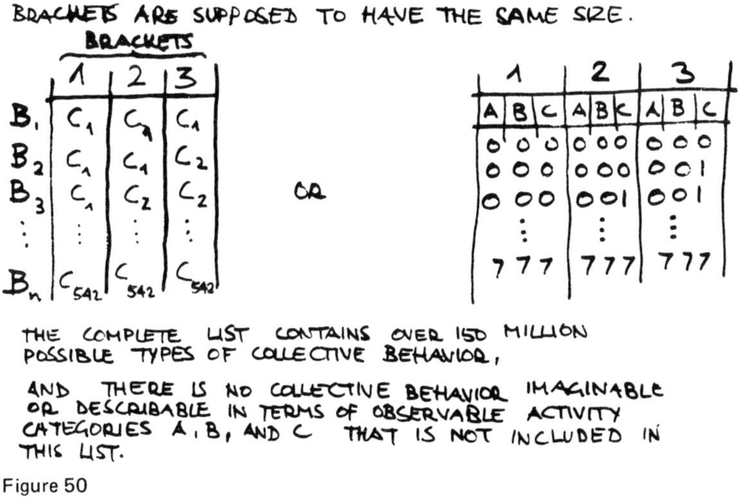

A LIST OF ALL TYPES OF COLLECTIVE BEHAVIOR B_i,
BASED ON OBSERVABLE ACTIVITY TYPES A, B AND C, AND
ON FREQUENCIES WITH WHICH THEY ARE PERFORMED
RANGING 1 THROUGH 7 (REFERENCE PERIOD: A WEEK).

THE COLLECTIVITY TO WHICH THE LIST REFERS IS
CONSIDERED AS CONTAINING 3 BRACKETS, EACH
HAVING ITS CHARACTERISTIC BEHAVIOR PATTERN.

BRACKETS ARE SUPPOSED TO HAVE THE SAME SIZE.

BRACKETS		
1	2	3
C_1	C_1	C_1
C_1	C_1	C_2
C_1	C_2	C_2
$\vdots$	$\vdots$	$\vdots$
C_{542}	C_{542}	C_{542}

(B₁, B₂, B₃, ..., Bₙ labels on rows)

OR

1			2			3		
A	B	C	A	B	C	A	B	C
0	0	0	0	0	0	0	0	0
0	0	0	0	0	0	0	0	1
0	0	0	0	0	1	0	0	1
$\vdots$		$\vdots$		$\vdots$				
7	7	7	7	7	7	7	7	7

THE COMPLETE LIST CONTAINS OVER 150 MILLION
POSSIBLE TYPES OF COLLECTIVE BEHAVIOR,

AND THERE IS NO COLLECTIVE BEHAVIOR IMAGINABLE
OR DESCRIBABLE IN TERMS OF OBSERVABLE ACTIVITY
CATEGORIES A, B, AND C THAT IS NOT INCLUDED IN
THIS LIST.

Figure 50

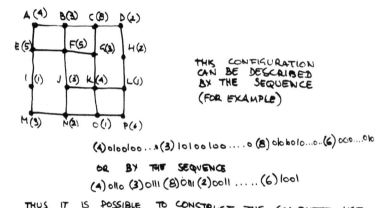

Figure 51

This list, like the preceding one (Section 5.2) can easily be constructed by judiciously adjusting the values of n and k to the possibilities of today's computers.

5.4 THE REFERENCE MATRIX: A DEFINITIVE INSTRUMENT FOR THE CITY PLANNING LABORATORY

Thus, in our preceding discussion, we have covered all considerations for constructing two complete lists (the field of reference, as we called it in Section 5.1):

a. The list of all possible types of behavior, based upon any types of activities belonging to categories A, B, and C.

b. The list of all possible weight distributions in all possible networks supported by n points.

It is clear that if we can form pairs that include one term from each of these lists, such pairs will constitute the precise description of a city, both as a mechanism and as a social entity.

In order to form these pairs, we must add a restriction in advance: this city has a definite population. The sum of the weights (number of arrivals), which is necessarily a multiple of the total number of inhabitants and which depends on the number of units in the time of reference, and the sum of all the fractions of the population carrying on a given activity (a sum which necessarily corresponds to the population) must be coordinate.

If we call j the sum of the frequencies of one type of collective behavior within the time span referred to; h, the number of categories of activities; b, the number of fractions; and p, the number of persons included in a fraction, we shall be able to establish the following constraint:

$$\sum_{z=1}^{z=n} w_z = p \cdot j \cdot h \cdot b, \sum_p = P$$

This constraint assures us that the two descriptions of the same city (description as a configuration and as collective behavior) are not contradictory (that is, there is a corresponding pair that includes a term from each of the two lists).

Thus, for each pair, there will be a specific value p, which can be calculated. If we assign a fixed value to p, there will be terms in the two lists which together cannot form a "type of city." Therefore, we shall necessarily select all the pairs which, satisfying this constraint, can be formed using terms from the two lists.

Having thus constructed all the possible pairs of urban mechanisms and corresponding types of behavior, we can obviously establish for each mechanism the "global effort" related to it (Section 3.3):

$$e = \sum_{x=1}^{x=n} \sum_{z=1}^{z=n} d_{xz} \cdot w_z \tag{1}$$

Without exception, the following condition must be filled for all these mechanisms:

$$\sum_{z=1}^{z=n} w_z = p \cdot j \cdot h \cdot b \tag{2}$$

Inevitably (the conditions imply it) every mechanism admitted is likely to form pairs with a great number of types of behavior, and, inversely, every type of behavior can be associated with a great number of mechanisms. We can represent all the mechanisms and all the types of behavior in the form of a matrix, putting, for example, all the types of behavior in the principal row of this matrix, well-ordered, since they result from combinatorial operations, and putting in the principle column of the matrix (Section 5.2) all the "mechanisms" (the distributions of weights in space) in the order stemming from the combinatorial operations that produced them (Section 5.3).

Within the field of this matrix (the field of reference) we can note a zero for any pair (mechanism and type of behavior) which does not satisfy condition (2), and inscribe the appropriate value of e (1) for the pairs that fulfill it. Thus there will be, for each term representing a configuration, a row containing values of e in positions (columns) corresponding to the types of behavior accepted as pairing off with this particular configuration (mechanism) since they fulfill condition (2), and zeroes in the positions belonging to the columns for types of behavior not accepted as forming these pairs. Inversely, in each column of the matrix corresponding to a given "type of behavior," there will be an appropriate value of e or a zero in the positions (rows) representing a configuration (a mechanism) fulfilling or not fulfilling condition (2) for this particular type of behavior.

This matrix is thus a simultaneous representation of all possible mechanisms and all the possible behaviors whether they exist or not, as well as representations of all possible global efforts (e) which characterize every urban organization resulting from a particular type of behavior within a given structure.

Next, this matrix reconstructs in a practical manner the field of reference of all possible histories of all possible organizations for cities. These histories may then be represented through

THE TWO COMPLETE LISTS:
1) OF ALL COLLECTIVE BEHAVIOR B_j
2) OF ALL POSSIBLE CONFIGURATIONS OF n POINTS D_i

MAKE IT POSSIBLE TO CONSTRUCT A MATRIX, WHICH,
FOR EVERY PAIR $D_i B_j$ SATISFYING THE EQUATION

$$\sum_{y=1}^{y=n} w_y = p \cdot j \cdot b$$

WHERE n = THE NUMBER OF POINTS IN THE NETWORK
w_y = WEIGHT OF POINT y
p = NUMBER OF PEOPLE IN A BRACKET
j = SUM OF FREQUENCIES CHARACTERIZING A COLLECTIVE BEHAVIOR
b = THE NUMBER OF BRACKETS

CONTAINS A GLOBAL EFFORT VALUE OF THE FORM

$$e_{ij} = \sum_{x=1}^{x=n} \sum_{y=1}^{y=n} d_{xy} \cdot w_y .$$

THIS GLOBAL EFFORT MATRIX, BASED ON COMPLETE LISTS OF
CONFIGURATIONS AND OF COLLECTIVE BEHAVIOR TYPES,
IS A <u>LABORATORY TOOL</u>.

Figure 52

THIS TOOL WILL LOOK LIKE THIS:

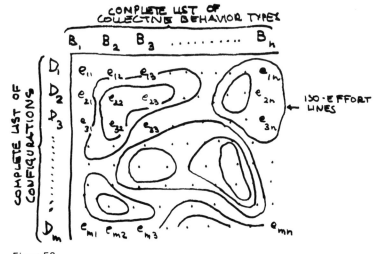

Figure 53

1. variations of weight distributions and configurations of infrastructures (mechanisms)

2. variations of types of behavior (distributions of activity of the total population of the city)

3. variations in the global effort parameter, which is an intrinsic and structural characteristic—however ill-defined—of a city.

The advantage of the crude values of the global effort parameter, in relation to the more detailed ones of local effort, lies in the fact that the number of possible cases, even choosing values as low as possible for n and k, would vastly exceed the capacity of a computer, if it had to store all the values of the local efforts in its memory. Therefore, it is only by calculating the local effort values solely as a "foregettable" subprogram, allowing for the calculation of global effort, that we can execute this program and remain within reasonable limits insofar as a computer's capacity is concerned.

5.5 POSSIBLE INTERRELATIONS AMONG HISTORIES

The practical importance of our matrix as a laboratory instrument comes from the opportunity it offers for comparing histories, be they abstract or observed.

Let us imagine, for example, a city organization corresponding to a well-defined pair in the matrix, on a given date in the history of that organization. At a later date, it will correspond to another pair in the matrix, later still to another, and so on. By its variations, the "actual history" will follow the plotting of three histories within the matrix (three histories mathematically independent of each other). These three histories will be the history of the configuration (vertical component), the history of behavior (horizontal component), and the history of global effort (the plotted curve itself). These three histories will all be accurately represented *in the same system of reference.*

We cannot guess in advance whether or not a regularity exists between two or three of these histories that may constitute a law of nature; but if one does exist, this matrix seems to be the best instrument for allowing us to detect it.

What facilitates the detection of a law, first of all, is the possibility of plotting, within the matrix, the curve of a relatively long history for a great number of existing city organizations simultaneously. Statistical records allow us in effect to reconstitute the history of most cities over a period of about fifty years, given that the numerical values that we need for this research are very "global" (approximate). By representing the tripartite history of all these city organizations, we shall obtain certain curves on the matrix, and the appearance of a regularity on one or several of these curves can be a key to the discovery of a "law of nature." If, on the other hand, we did not find any law of this sort, that would mean that city organizations (taking into account that our knowledge of them is limited) are not subject to laws of the determinist type, but that we must look for laws of chance.

For better legibility we shall represent this matrix not in the form of a simple numerical table, but, as we did in the case of effort maps, graphically by means of a chart of "iso-global effort" lines which will show the regions in which values for e belong to the same "bracket" (the same fraction).

The first regularity (or absence of regularity) will be distribution of the lines of iso-global effort themselves. This regularity cannot be foreseen, or even assumed, until the matrix is constructed in its entirety. For if the iso-global effort lines in the local effort maps follow, in a predictable manner, the example of other models of the "distribution of potential" type, by contrast the iso-global effort curves of our matrix will not correspond to any known real model. We would therefore have to look for some surprises.

It may be that the iso-global effort lines will show the regularity or the nonregularity of the e parameter. But we can also detect other regularities within the two "complete lists" themselves: first of all, equivalencies, that is, the same "configuration" functioning in the same manner (and thus having the same value for e) with very different types of behavior, or even the same type of behavior functioning in the same manner (the same value for e) within different physical configurations.

To carry this experimentation further, we can represent the history of

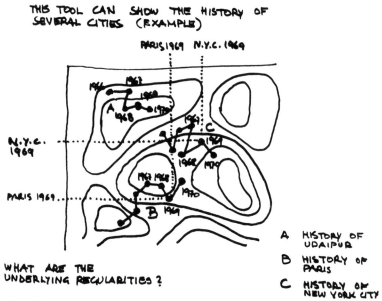

THIS TOOL CAN SHOW THE HISTORY OF
SEVERAL CITIES (EXAMPLE)

PARIS 1969   N.Y.C. 1969

A   HISTORY OF
    UDAIPUR

B   HISTORY OF
    PARIS

C   HISTORY OF
    NEW YORK CITY

WHAT ARE THE
UNDERLYING REGULARITIES ?

Figure 54

cities in the matrix; then, each time that the curve of a history shows
certain characteristic traits (peaks, inflections, and so on) seek out the
corresponding events in the actual history of the cities. We would thus
be able to discover whether or not certain characteristics of the history
of the mechanism correspond to certain types of events rather than to
others; however, the discovery of such relationships would be more a
surprise to me than an anticipated fact, for I am very suspicious of the
sort of intuitive explanations by which events are generally interpreted.

   Therefore, we see that the construction of this matrix could be the
appropriate tool for a large number of experiments with models, and
that it would certainly lead us to a better understanding of the "natural
laws" of city planning, if such laws really exist.

   Naturally, in addition to functioning as a tool for experimentation,
this matrix could also be used as a tool for planning. Let us suppose
that a city planner, working for a given society that has a definite type
of behavior, has to propose a certain number of planning alternatives.

The type of behavior of this society can be easily coded by an observer who will note, in categories *A, B,* and *C,* the frequency with which certain activities, decided on in advance, are pursued. Once the type of behavior has been defined, the city planner has only to look at the matrix for all the configurations (mechanisms) having a value *e* of global effort less than or equal to a threshold value arbitrarily chosen and considered to be desirable. Thus the matrix—unlike "optimization" models—provides an answer by selecting a set of equivalent solutions (equivalent as to the global effort value that characterizes the mechanism), instead of a single and unique "best" solution.

This is how the matrix can be put to use by the "physical planner" (the urban planner, the builder). But there is a symmetrical path open to the "social planner": in his case, the physical configuration (the mechanism) constitutes the observable datum (the network and the distribution of termini within). Once he has observed the existing configuration and situated it in the matrix, the social planner can search this matrix for all types of behavior not carrying the sign 0 which, when paired with the configuration in question, give a value *e* of global effort less than or equal to a value arbitrarily determined in advance as a desirable threshold.

Thus, this "tool" makes it possible to find, depending on the need at hand, a set of solutions applicable to a given situation, with perfectly predictable effects: either material configurations to be applied to a particular social situation, or social improvements to be made in a given physical context.

5.6 POSSIBLE CATEGORIES OF OBSERVABLE ACTIVITIES AND THEIR INTERPRETATIONS

The matrix defined above could be an indispensable tool for another kind of research: research on significant categories of activities.

As I showed earlier, the matrix constitutes a "mapping field" for possible relationships between the distributions of termini (mechanisms) and types of behavior as defined by certain categories of activities.

The distributions of termini within a network are "hard" (concrete) data, which anyone can observe and, as the terminus characteristics contained in these data account only for the situation of a terminus in the network and its weight of attraction, these observations will be the same whoever the observer happens to be.

Types of behavior are also hard data: the frequency of activity plotted during a fixed time of reference can be observed by anyone in the same manner.

The only "soft" element (as in "software"), and therefore the only one that is arbitrarily chosen, is the set of "distinctive signs" by which activities are taken as belonging to the same or to different categories. Indeed, the matrix, which operates on abstract activities A, B, and C, never has any direct connection with these signs.

Moreover, in our matrix, all the histories based on categories of activities A, B, and C, whatever the distinctive signs under which they are observed, can be plotted simultaneously. Certain of them will show regularities, others will not. For example, if we give the meanings of "work," "leisure," and "supply" to categories A, B, and C, or if we translate them by "activities raising blood pressure," "not changing blood pressure," or "decreasing blood pressure," the frequency distributions, and consequently the histories obtained and their eventual regularities, will doubtless be very different.

One of the problems of sociology lies precisely in this tacitly arbitrary choice of categories of activity (work, leisure, supply, for example). I do not see how a mere spectator could recognize, when an "observed" person pursues an activity, to what category this activity belongs, and I do not even see that these categories are complementary (and consequently that the list is complete). These categories are, therefore, a completely arbitrary set, often the results of the semantic abuses of a given civilization, and they are certainly not suited to projecting solutions, or to the study of solutions in changing society. (Moreover, these semantic preconceptions are one reason for extreme intolerance in every society).

In any case, in the matrix under discussion, we can represent the image of an observed history, with the aid of several constructed (mapped) histories, whose interpretation is based on different categories of activities, defined by different distinctive signs. The "historical curves" which will result, even if they are different, will certainly have at least one point in common: they will all refer to exactly the same sequence of "actual" observed events, which they all represent, by means of different modes of observation. One could certainly discover a regularity among the different curves themselves, or between those curves and the general distribution of values for e (global effort), or among any sets of data in the matrix.

If it were possible to detect certain of these relationships (regularities), we would have a fundamental "law of nature" for sociology, a law of which we are yet unaware, and for which we may have great need.

Thus, for the sociologist (or for the specialist in group dynamics), the matrix proposed here offers the hope of finally having an experimental tool.

If, in the primitive state of affairs which presently obtains, the city planner hopes for the aid of the sociologist in finding a way out of his critical situation, in the future it may well be the city planner who rescues the sociologist by providing him with both the tools and the observations.

CHAPTER 6 THE CITY

6.1 THE PRIVATE CITY

I live in Paris, which is a very large city of eight million inhabitants. Of course, to say that I live in Paris does not mean that I come into daily or even yearly contact with all these people. In reality I encounter in the city about two thousand persons in all. Among these, there are about twenty-five that I see every week, fifty that I see every two weeks, and so on. The set of people whom I actually encounter, with varying regularity, constitutes what I call my "private city." So in effect I do not live in Paris, but in my "private city"; and I would only be aware of people leaving Paris if they belonged to this "private city."

There are eight million of these private cities in Paris, since each inhabitant has his own. Each "private city" represents a linkage scheme, that is, the graph of the movements of an inhabitant making use of the real infrastructure of the real city. This implies the existence of a great number of crossovers, about $8,000,000^4$, or 4×10^{27}. Since each crossover represents a "source of potential conflict," such a number signifies that I am living on a volcano!

The number of potential conflicts resulting from the peaceful coexistence of a very large number of private cities is far too great for any presently existing computer to manipulate. The problem of knowning how a city functions is nowhere near solved, even in its simplest form, and, except for the general application described in the previous chapter, we must rule out the method of using a complete list, because of the dimensions it may assume.

It is obvious that this complexity should prevent the observer (or the city planner or the architect) from bringing to the problem a solution

THE REAL CITY IS AN INFRASTRUCTURE
CONTAINING A PRIVATE CITY FOR EACH INHABITANT

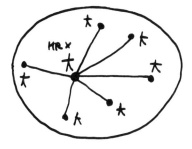

MR X'S PRIVATE CITY
CONTAINS ALL THE PEOPLE
MR X VISITS
DURING A PERIOD OF
REFERENCE

Figure 55

THE REAL CITY IS AN INEXTRICABLE
NETWORK OF PRIVATE CITIES.

EACH OF THESE PRIVATE CITIES
IS VERY IMPORTANT TO ITS "CREATOR".

IF A CROSSOVER IN A CITY
CAN BE INTERPRETED
AS A SOURCE OF POTENTIAL
CONFLICT
THEN A CITY OF THE SIZE
OF PARIS (8 MILLION INHABITANTS)
CREATES $4 \cdot 10^{27}$ CONFLICT
SOURCES.

THAT IS A VERY LARGE NUMBER.

Figure 56

based on a system of his own private values and affirming that such and such a "private city" is preferable to all the others (the optimization method). Now, this manner of judging the "value" of different private cities (that is, different modes of living) is one of the gravest abuses, even if unconscious, that a city planner commits, since it is a matter of individual opinions, where no comparisons are possible.

However, if the city planner absolutely has not, and cannot have, any moral right to make decisions concerning someone else's private city, he can still act as a "counsellor." The model of the urban mechanism, described in the preceding two chapters, in effect allows him to inform each person of the consequences he may expect, both for himself and for others, from living in such and such a "private city." The city planner himself cannot perform this task of warning each inhabitant individually, but the inhabitant himself can be prepared, during his primary schooling, to calculate these consequences on his own.

I should therefore propose teaching children, at the age of eight or ten, to become accustomed to the "play" of a city: I mean "playing" and not "playing a game," for we have seen that game theory does not apply to cities (there are no "rules of the game," and certainly no final outcome like the one that a "game," according to game theory, is supposed to have). "Playing" here means simulating a system within which the acts of others exert a definable influence on our own acts. I am not a teacher, but I do not believe that it would be too difficult to represent an "infrastructure," for example, by a certain number of chairs (let us say two chairs per child). and to let the children group themselves on the chairs as they wish, in order to perform the activities they like. Children also have their "private cities," and one might give them explanations that they could easily visualize: for example, of the intrinsic characteristics of configurations that they have instinctively chosen for themselves.

6.2 PROBLEMS BECOME MEANINGFUL ONLY IF WE HAVE ADEQUATE INFORMATION: THE INFRASTRUCTURE AS MEDIUM

The impossibility of finding solutions for all the conflicts brought

about by the existence of a large number of "private cities" results
from the extreme paucity of information obtainable about each "private city." Therefore, the first proposals mentioned in the preceding
section were (1) to find a simple way to code information concerning
private cities; (2) to teach the individual user to read this code.

Once the information has been made readable and has been read, it
allows a comparison among several possibilities. And the comparison
will give an individual user the means of profiting from his information
about his private city within a physical structure by finding the solution that he prefers, for he can find it only if he is familiar with all the
alternatives at his disposal, even in simplified form, that is, with a complete list of possible solutions.

We cannot compare the solutions contained in this complete list if
they do not have a certain frame of reference in common; moreover,
frames of reference are more convenient when they can refer to a larger
set of possible solutions.

I have given the name "infrastructures" to these frames of reference
which can be used for all possible solutions. An infrastructure may thus
contain all the "private cities" (imaginable or existing) which I spoke
about earlier. In a preceding chapter we saw that the physical form of
an infrastructure is generally a network, for which rules of utilization
have been established (we saw several examples of these in Chapter 4).

An infrastructure is composed, therefore, of a *network + rules.* Consequently, city planners as well as users are intensely concerned with
infrastructures and their rules of use. Once the common rules for using
a network are established, any user can have his private rules. We would
regard the best common rules are those which conflict the least with
private rules.

We can state this principle in another way, by saying that an infrastructure must be as "uncommitted" ("neutral") as possible, that is,
conceived with the individual user in mind, with the end of satisfying
his preferences, whatever they may be.

I stress this statement because it contradicts a highbrow superstition
which would have us believe that a city's "personality" must lie in its
arrangement and form. It is, in fact, a grave mistake: indeed, the less

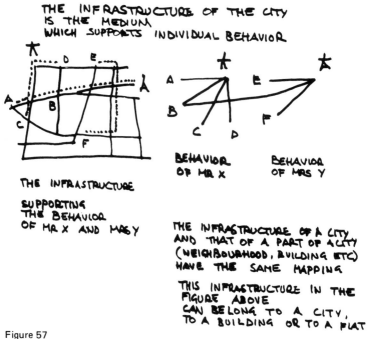

Figure 57

personality the "hardware" of a city has, the more possible it is for its inhabitants to have their own. The city *is* its inhabitants, and the physical city without inhabitants is nothing but a ruin.

Since the beginning of the book, I have insisted, first and foremost, that information processes should be involved in city planning. After all the theoretical and general reflections which have been necessary, we can now consider this fact as evident: *the infrastructure is the principal medium of information of a city,* in the sense that a medium conveys a message: the infrastructure is the medium and the usage schemes are the messages. The usage schemes (private cities) superimposed on this infrastructure *are* the real city.

6.3 THE INFRASTRUCTURE MUST FULFILL CERTAIN CONDITIONS

There are two categories of "private cities" superimposed on the infrastructure:

1. the "private" private city, used by an inhabitant most of the time: his personal environment (flat, apartment, house, room).

2. the "public" private city, used less often by the inhabitant during a given time of reference: his "errands network" (social life, public obligations, trips for no particular purpose, and so on).

The difference between these two categories is solely quantitative: the "private" private city is the one that we use every day, and the "public" private city the one we use less frequently. Naturally, the "private private city" of one person can be the "public private city" of another. (For example, if I am invited to someone's home for a drink, my "public" private city coincides with his "private" private city.)

We do not use the "private" private city of another person as if it were our own; on the other hand, several "public" private cities can have intersections or even be identical. A given place in the city can belong to several of these "public" private cities; for example, in Paris, the waiting room at the Gare Saint-Lazare, where I go to meet my girlfriend, rather than to catch a train.

The physical infrastructure (hardware) of the city must consequently fulfill the following conditions:

1. An inhabitant must be able to have, within the infrastructure, the "private" city he prefers for himself, whatever its nature. (He must thus be able to choose, according to his preferences, the cost of his home and his situation within the infrastructure.)

2. He must be informed of the consequences of his choice as far as cost and situation are concerned, and also of the consequences of other people's choices: therefore the infrastructure's role as frame of reference (infrastructure = network + rules) must be clearly established.

3. An inhabitant must subsequently be able to modify any decision and every implementation of his choice (cost and site of his home): the infrastructure must allow for "mobility." (N. B. Since 1957, I have been using the term "mobile architecture" for any solution allowing users to make a direct decision and transform their environments directly as soon as they decided to reconsider and modify their previous decisions. The term, which seemed somewhat exaggerated when it was first used

(and which I had chosen for want of a better one) today has become a generally accepted expression in professional jargon, and even time-honored to the point where is has transcended my personal jargon.)

6.4 THE INFRASTRUCTURE IS NOT THE CITY

In one of the preceding chapters, we saw that every n graph, including the complete graph, could be plotted on the saturated n graph (which constitutes its support). If we consider the activities of the inhabitants (which are symbolized by their "private cities") as a less connected graph than the one representing the physical infrastructure of the city, which supports the *other* graph, the "real" city will consist, for us, of "hardware" (physical infrastructure) and the modes of use within this infrastructure.

This statement shows clearly why the expressions "urban design" and "urban planning" are so devoid of meaning: it shows us how utopian it is to hope to find someone capable of projecting or planning modes of use, or even specialized physical constructions intended for certain modes of use, real but not detected or detectable. This same statement leads us to the observation that the only logical act for an architect or city planner must consist of designing the most "neutral" physical infrastructures possible in relation to modes of use.

I settled this problem in an earlier section of this book by proposing, first of all, sets of points "with the minimum number of connections" or "with the maximum number of connections" (Section 3.4); then, any planar network of homogeneous degree (Section 4.2) as an appropriate mapping for infrastructures.

6.5 AN EXAMPLE OF THE INFRASTRUCTURE AS "HARDWARE": THE "SPATIAL CITY"

Just as an example, I am now going to try to describe to you an infrastructure which I created in 1958 and used for different projects, most of which have been widely published in professional journals.

This project was based on two sets of criteria, the first comprising general criteria for infrastructures, the second made up of economic considerations relating to the context.

Let us draw up the list of these two groups of criteria:

The first set (1) concerns economy of use. The principle has been to reduce use efforts, such as time lost or dissatisfaction due to the pre-established and imposed modes of use, contrary to the personal habits of the real user, and so on.

1a. The infrastructure must be the most "neutral" possible network, interfering as little as possible with arbitrarily chosen modes of use applied within it.

1b. The infrastructure must contain the fewest possible potential conflicts (crossovers).

1c. The infrastructure is the *only fixed physical element* of the city: all the other "hardware" (elements inserted into the infrastructure, floors, ceilings, walls, partitions, fixtures, and so on) as well as nonphysical elements (movements of people, climate, visual aspects, and others) are interchangeable, transformable, movable: they are in effect "mobile" and can be adapted to any particular mode of use.

1d. The infrastructure requires a minimum of "safety" regulations, providing for the elimination of mutually disruptive or contradictory modes of use.

The most important of these regulations concerns the relation between height (and therefore minimum clearance for windows) and the "coefficient of surface use" (the corresponding formula is given in Figure 58).

The second set of criteria (2) concerns economy of construction.

2a. Construction of the infrastructure must fulfill all the criteria of set (1) concerning economy of use.

2b. Construction of the infrastructure must impose the fewest possible elements of new or specialized construction, and must take advantage of preexisting conditions.

2c. Construction must economize as much as possible on the costliest elements in a given context: manpower on construction sites and transport (raw material and manufacture being the least costly elements).

These two sets of criteria led me to the following solution:

1a. The infrastructure must be a planar network of homogeneous degree or the "spatialization" (through labeling) of a network of this type.

PARAMETERS OF USE

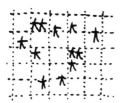

CLASSICAL CONCEPT
OF POPULATION DENSITY:
NUMBER OF PEOPLE
PER UNIT OF SPACE

SAME OCCUPANCY PATTERN:

AN ADMITTED MINIMUM DISTANCE
BETWEEN DIFFERENT OCCUPANCIES
IS THE PARAMETER

$+b+d+b+d_2+b+ d_3 +b+d_4 +b+$

THE NUMBER OF LEVELS
(MULTIPLICATION OF THE
GROUND SURFACE)
IS LIMITED BY THE
INCIDENCE ANGLE OF
NATURAL LIGHT.

THE COEFFICIENT OF GROUND
SURFACE MULTIPLICATION
CAN BE MEASURED BY THE
RELATION OF THE TOTAL AREA
OF ALL SURFACES (GROUND INCLUDED) (S_T)
AND THE AREA OF THE ORIGINAL
GROUND SURFACE (S_o).

THE EQUATION OF THIS COEFFICIENT
IN THE CASE OF n LEVELS IS

$$E_n = \frac{S_T}{S_o} = \frac{2n}{n+1} < 2 \text{ FOR ALL } n.$$

Figure 58

1b. This network must be, if possible, a planar homogeneous network of fourth degree or the "spatialization" of this network.

1c. The physical infrastructure must be of the "skeleton" type (represented by the graph with the maximum number of connections), not of the "troglodyte" type.

1d. The number of levels of the infrastructure must equal at least 4 and at most 8 if one bears in mind the minimum clearance for windows and the building heights currently permitted in Europe or America.

2a. The infrastructure corresponding to the criteria of set (1) must be a continuous multistory skeletal construction comprising 4 to 8 levels. The beams and/or columns that constitute the skeleton must contain all the supply and disposal lines so that no space in the skeleton lacks a connection or outlet for any kind of line (electricity, water, drainage).

2b. As in European or American locations (for which these projects were designed), where spaces of essentially two sizes are used, the spaces in our infrastructure belong to two categories: the small spaces, characterized by a small use load (offices, apartments, hospitals, schools), and the large spaces, with a large use load (public meeting places, warehouses, stores, garages, industrial sites). We call the first type "cellular" and the second type "communal." It makes sense to locate the "communal" spaces; with their large volumes and their heavy use loads, at the ground level of the infrastructure (the earth's surface being the least costly of the structures capable of supporting a heavy load), and to assign "cellular use" to the small spaces within the skeletal part of the infrastructure, above ground level.

2c. The two most expensive operations in construction are site work and transport. So the infrastructure must be constructed of easily transportable materials, and it should be assembled with the least possible work at the site.

The infrastructure which I then proposed was conceived as a spatial framework in which the total height of all the levels together was the construction height (that is, height upon which the construction's load-bearing depends); the resistance of this increased construction height made it possible to span the large spaces situated at ground level. The

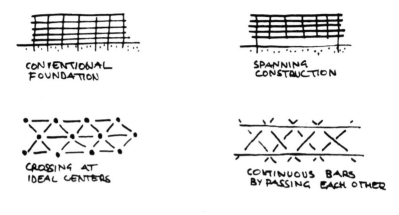

CONVENTIONAL
FOUNDATION

SPANNING
CONSTRUCTION

CROSSING AT
IDEAL CENTERS

CONTINUOUS BARS
BY PASSING EACH OTHER

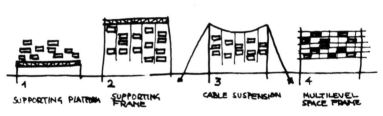

1
SUPPORTING PLATFORM

2
SUPPORTING
FRAME

3
CABLE SUSPENSION

4
MULTILEVEL
SPACE FRAME

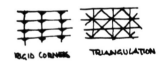

RIGID CORNERS

TRIANGULATION

Figure 59

HYPERBOLIC PARABOLOID

HYPERBOLOID
OF ROTATION
(ONE SHEET)

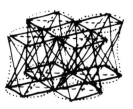

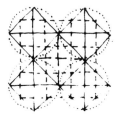

Figure 59, continued

structure included triangulated beams, whose constituent bars crossed
the structure from end to end and were attached by collar joints. The
spatial framework had been chosen so that the empty spaces within the
structure corresponded to the cellular spaces, and so that between two
cellular spaces there were the fewest possible diagonals in the separating
plane (such diagonals obstruct potential passages). Finally, there was to
be no diagonal, or any other beam, within the spaces themselves.

   All these spatial structures can be developed according to a simple
archetype, which assembles hyperboloids of rotation of a single surface;
the beams then coincide with two families of straight lines plotted on
these surfaces (although the latter do not exist physically) using points
of a planar network of homogeneous degree.

6.6 MODIFYING A CHOICE CARRIED OUT WITHIN THE INFRASTRUCTURE

The arrangement resulting from applying one or several choices and implementing them within the infrastructure can become unsatisfactory
for one reason or another. In that case, it will be necessary for the individual user (or group of users) who have made that choice to be able
to modify the arrangement. It will always be possible to carry out this

modification if all the elements inserted in the infrastructure are *mobile,* and if the infrastructure remains the only *fixed* physical component of the city. As we have already seen, this material component must be designed to permit any imaginable arrangement, that is to say, any labeled linkage scheme of a collection of n distinct elements included in a complete list (repertoire). Once the project has been set up in this manner, there is no chance of obstacles to any imaginable modification except perhaps for the conservatism of the users.

As the modifications can lead from any possible arrangement (labeled, connected planar n graph) contained in the complete list to any other, and as no correction can lead to an arrangement not contained in the list (since only physically or geometrically impossible arrangements are not recorded in it), the corrections can set off an endless cyclical process: no one arrangement is "better" than the others, except in a given context where great narrow-mindedness would prevail. But I cannot imagine that such a context, if it existed, would long obtain, and consequently there is no final solution foreseeable for this cyclical chain of corrections, and no arrangement that is absolutely "best."

One implication of this conclusion is that "game theory" cannot be used to describe urban affairs, since by definition this theory must operate toward a "final state" (when one of the partners wins; or, in the case of a tie, toward an indecisive final situation). An endless game is meaningless, and game theory cannot be applied to unending processes, since all its evaluations are based on the end of the game; for example, how to reach the end the fastest, or how to terminate the game under given conditions, whatever they may be. So I do not see any meaning to the question: "How can you end an endless game?"

The use of a city is not a game that follows game theory.

Let us return to the example of the user of the "Flatwriter" (see Section 3.7). Let us imagine that one regulation of the infrastructure obliges all users to leave an empty space for each space used within the structure; in other words, that only 50 percent of the available places in the infrastructure will be sold.

From that premise, the first user to choose the site for his personal environment in the infrastructure seems to have the most freedom of choice, and the last user seems to have the least freedom of choice. In reality, the situation is exactly reversed: the first user has chosen his site with the greatest liberty as regards his geogrphic situation, but he has the least influence on who his neighbors will be. Every person making a choice after him can become his neighbor. On the other hand, the last one to choose can become the neighbor of any group, according to his preferences. From the viewpoint of his "private city," he has the greatest freedom of choice.

But, since the modification process is endless, there is no "last to choose." For example, the first user will be able to modify his choice once the last one has made his, and he will be able to choose a location where he will have friends that he prefers. After that another user can make a similar modification, and this can continue endlessly. Thus no one can predict what arrangement this chain of modification will tend toward in the end.

Thus the infrastructure, appropriately chosen, makes possible the birth of the "indeterminate city" (which already exists today, but in a latent form). The fact of giving it an infrastructure allows this dynamic city to attain the characteristic rhythm of change appropriate to it.

Thus the city will become a sort of random configuration.

APPENDIX TO CHAPTER 6: NEW PROBLEMS IN THE INDUSTRIALIZATION OF CONSTRUCTION

1. THE GENERAL CONTEXT

The world situation shows very different characteristics from that of a decade ago: we are witnessing the passage of our world from a period of local affluence to one of generalized scarcity.

Indeed, the known energy reserve is considered sufficient for at most fifteen years, and the time span necessary for the development of new sources of energy is estimated by the experts as at least twice as long. This points to a period of energy scarcity of fifteen to twenty years.

World food reserves are insufficient to assure survival for more than one year. If we happen to have two consecutive drought years in Asia (which happens generally once every twenty-five years), food might be scarce all over the world (famines are no longer local as they were in the nineteenth century). We have no hope even of setting up some central organization to coordinate measures to deal with these emerging menaces: indeed, communication necessarily breaks down within organizations larger than a certain "natural threshold." The disintegration of large organizations (which are considered by Western-type civilizations to be unique guarantees against poverty) accelerates the processes of general impoverishment.

It is urgent that industry, agriculture, and organizations become aware of this deterioration of the global situation, but obviously it is easier to write about it than to do something. The tremendous inertia of human habits, the interest of ruling groups in continuing the exploitation of existing technological setups, and the difficulty of communication make it impossible for any warning to be efficient within short range. We are thus sitting in a "spaceship" whose steering does not function any more, heading for a crash. The best we can do is to make this crash softer.

To do so, we would need to find some new ways
1. of using less energy and fewer raw materials
2. of reducing food consumption to the biologically necessary level instead of wasting food as we do today
3. of adapting technology for relatively small groups, who would produce on a relatively small scale, instead of mass-production technology, which involves mass transportation, loss of individuality, and so on.

We can presume that civilizations that do not adapt themselves to this course might have a very reduced chance of survival.

2. PARTICULAR CONTEXT OF BUILDING INDUSTRIALIZATION

I had to open with this review because the trend I have described determines the future for the field of construction. This future seems to be somewhat less dark than that of most industries, simply because building industry is still not committed to any definite technology and thus alternative ways are still open.

The problems, which will be the subject of this appendix, have to do with these alternatives.

What features should the new building technology have?
1. Let us begin with the energy problem: building technology should *consume the least energy possible.* A building should "cost" minimal energy, both in assembly (in the factory and in situ) and in transport. For example, one square yard of wood construction consumes less energy than one square yard of steel structure, which in turn is "energy-cheaper" than a square yard of reinforced concrete building.

Let us presume, that in order to determine "energy costs," we could introduce a parameter indicating for any building technology the proportion "applied energy"/"lifetime of the construction." Such a parameter could give useful hints as to which technologies are to be favored.
2. "Lifetime" of a building means the time span in which it can be used efficiently in any way which should be determined by its users. If users cannot use a building any more in their own way, the building can be considered as "dead" even if it is not a ruin or demolished. (Many

buidlings today are "still-born."

A corollary to this statement would be that in order for a building to "live," its space allocation, the connection schemes between its spaces, its organization, what we call generally its "plan," *must be determined by its future users.*

3. Another corollary to our statement about the "lifetime" of a building is that *the user should be able to perform all repairs himself.* Indeed, we see that a large number of buildings decay very fast, because the technology used to construct them does not admit simple repairs, and there is no regular servicing to perform repair jobs requiring skill.

4. The organization which would produce construction elements which fulfill these conditions (low energy consumption in the production process, adaptability to plans conceived by the user, ease of repair for the unskilled handyman) must be necessarily a *relatively small organization,* between industrial and artisanal size.

This desideratum follows both from the "low-energy condition" (as small production plants working for regional markets need less energy and less transportation than large ones), and from the "low-production" condition (small amounts of very varied stock elements permit a bigger selection than very large amounts of uniform elements).

Beside these particular reasons, smaller industrial plants are called for as well by the general context: the communication breakdown I mentioned before is essentially unfavorable to large organizations.

5. A last, but not the least important, desideratum for the new type of industrialization process for buildings concerns the *"agglomeration characteristics"* implied by these technologies.

Let me explain this concept. If, for example, a technology does not admit the construction of individual low-rise buildings, or that of collective high-rise buildings, such a technology produces a constraint for collective use, urban design, and so on. Other consequences of constraints resulting from the implementation of a technology might concern: distances between buildings, use of ground surface, use of overhead space. Such constraints also influence traffic patterns and land use characteristics. Appliances might have effects on utilization patterns (for example, certain appliances involve community use, others favor individual use as it is in the case of heating appliances or washing devices. These constraints are what I call the "agglomeration characteristics" of technological objects.

It is not enough to say that a technology such as that described in Chapter 6 will make possible any plan and any design. It is necessary to encourage the user about his own capacity both as designer and repairman. It is necessary to give him the tools, analytical or material, to act as such. It is necessary to make him understand that he himself is the only "expert" who can solve his own problems, and that he should trust himself more than he trusts other "experts."

3. CONCLUSION

I have sketched, by intention, a very radical image of new trends in building industrialization. The trends I mentioned imply, even more than a transformation of technology, a transformation of attitude.

There is a growing resistance among professionals (architects, engineers, builders) *against* such a change of attitude. There is—as I tried to point out—a growing pressure in favor of a new attitude among users, a pressure resulting from emerging conditions in the world context.

I think that a new trend is necessary and feasible (feasible, because building industralization is still not so developed that it will not admit reorganization). But when I say "necessary," I mean that the alternative trend should completely supplant classical techniques and attitudes. I think that both trends should coexist until a time when a tradeoff equilibrating the two tendencies becomes possible. In order to reach this situation, we have to work on the new trend, which has research priority (the classical trend does not need it: it exists already). It is the task of research to develop what does not exist but is imminent.

CHAPTER 7 SOME CONCLUSIONS ABOUT SOCIETY

7.1 THE NONCOMPETITIVE SOCIETY

There is certainly no lack of prophecies and projections today. And yet, a new and absolutely unprecedented form of society is developing before our eyes, ignored by most of the prophecies.

I am going to try to describe it, not in the form of a prediction but as a way of demonstrating how inadequate our imagination and intuition are even when it comes to picturing so imminent a reality.

We all agree that survival demands a continual struggle for most (if not all) living creatures. It is evident that this struggle takes the form of a competitive game, with rules that vary according to the species, wherein the loser "loses" the right to survive.

We also know that this struggle for survival affects only the areas where a certain means of survival is not available to a species in sufficient quantities. An arid region, for example, where all the animals struggle for possesion of a water site, is different from a country where water can be found practically everywhere. Another example: despite the primordial importance of oxygen, no animal struggles to obtain it. A first observation can be expressed thus: *competition among individuals of a species is a function of the scarcity of the means of survival.* This first observation is valid for every animal species.

A second observation follows, which is valid only for man and certain animals: *the scarcity of the means of survival can be natural or artificial* (that is, a part of the species can induce an artificial scarcity with the aim of imposing its will on the other part). All struggles, political or military, among human beings, are characterized by the efforts of one side to control one of the means of the other's survival. This observation

implies the existence of another ingenious device: if it is impossible to
introduce artificial scarcity of the real means of survivial, there is always
the possibility of inventing fictitious means. These fictitious means of
survival are provided by religions, group loyalties, various legal concepts,
and so on. Their essential characteristic lies in setting up a rule of preeminence.

Our epoch is approaching (in certain countries it has already reached)
sufficient supply of the absolutely necessary means of survivial. (Bread,
water, and so on no longer present problems, for example, in the
U. S. A.). These countries have therefore introduced "acute awareness
of preeminence" (status consciousness) into the scale of "public"
values and Americans today are struggling more for "status symbols"
than for anything else.

Yet there is this interesting but no less obvious fact: *the first signs of
a "noncompetitive" society appear precisely in these countries.* I am
thinking in particular all the tendencies called "hippie." It seems to
me that the outward signs of hippyism have only negligeable importance compared to the significance of the effort (perhaps unconscious)
to eliminate competition: refusal to work (to earn more money than
the necessary minimum), refusal to form competitive subgroups (non-
violence), sexual promiscuity (the sexual partner is one of the necessi-
ties of survival which, all through history, has been the most "artificially" scarce).

Despite the imminence of this development, neither I (an observer)
nor the hippies have the slightest idea of the form that a noncompetitive society would assume.

By way of example, I am going to try to construct a representation
(of course many representations differing from my example are possible).

A noncompetitive society (according to this picture) *could be nothing but a nonsociety.* Beginning with the fact that the ties between individuals are automatically linked to competition, this new "society"
leads us to conclude that a *noncompetitive society must take the form
of a group of individuals having no contact with each other.*

To us today as members of a classical type of society, it seems that the members of such a mutually indifferent society *would be bored to death.*

But this representation of society can lead us much further. First I am reminded of the strange metamorphosis of certain grasshoppers: for a long time, entomologists thought that there were two species of these grasshoppers ("solitary" and "gregarious") until the day they found that these two species were the same, and that the grasshopper *merely changed its physical aspect depending on whether it lived alone or in a group.* Could it be possible that man is a similar animal, that is, different depending on whether he lives in society or in isolation? If so, that would imply *that the noncompetitive society might involve a biological mutation of the human species.*

A strange observation comes to mind in this connection. For a long time, it has been known that longevity among the inhabitants of certain countries is more common than elsewhere. These countries (Bulgaria, Soviet Georgia, Iceland, and others) do not have many geographic characteristics in common, but *in all these countries men live in a very isolated, solitary way or in very small groups.* Is it, then, possible to say that perhaps noncompetitiveness, the solitary life, and longevity are not isolated facts? My brief reflections have led me far, much farther than I wished. The only thing that I really wanted to demonstrate is that the sociologist, the biologist, and the psychologist have neither valid expectations as to the development of life styles, nor even any imagination about the possibilities of development. All planning based on prognostics thus errs not on account of *too much* imagination but on account of *too little.* Admitting the possibility of cumulative errors, I am suspicious of methods based on intuition. *Any prediction that is not based on an axiomatics must be highly erroneous.* In the preceding sentences I gave an example of a line of reasoning intuitively constructed, whose truth or falsity cannot be demonstrated or even evaluated. In any case, I had fun doing it.

To be serious again, after this mere game of invention, I can admit that I came in the end to construct an axiomatics that shows (following the criteria specified earlier) that this noncompetitive type of society is *really* possible. The subject of this axiomatics is the function of "property." From the axiomatics, I constructed the complete combinatorial list that corresponds to it; then I interpreted each term in the list as a possible "society," and I added an *example* of a possible "society" from the different classes of possible "societies."

Axioms:

1. An individual can use an object

   A1: exclusively for himself

   B1: simultaneously with others

2. The attitude of the other individuals toward use of the object may vary

   A2: their consent and help are necessary

   B2: their consent and help are not necessary

3. The possibility of transferring the object varies

   A3: the object can be transferred to other individuals

   B3: the object cannot be transferred to other individuals

The complete combinatorial list constructed with the aid of this axiomatics takes the following form:

   A1 A2 A3: property exclusive, consent necessary, transfer possible (example: "classical" type of society)

   A1 A2 B3: property exclusive, consent necessary, transfer impossible (example: society based on prestige, a status society)

   A1 B2 A3: property exclusive, consent unnecessary, transfer possible (example: "primitive" type of society, based on violence)

   B1 B2 B3: property exclusive, consent unnecessary, transfer impossible (example: group of recluses)

   B1 A2 A3: property commonly owned, consent necessary, transfer possible (example: "collectivist" society)

   B1 A2 B3: property commonly owned, consent necessary, transfer impossible (example: noncompetitive society)

   B1 B2 A3: property commonly owned, consent unnecessary, transfer possible (example: a pack of animals)

   B1 B2 B3: property simultaneously owned, consent unnecessary, transfer impossible (example: religious community, "vegetative" society)

   I do not intend to pursue the entire analysis which can be developed from this list (that is, to set up a schema of transpositions of one term on the list to another). I shall be satisfied with saying that the noncompetitive society is possible and observable and that I wait with curiosity to see what form it will take.

7.2 CRISIS

We hear a lot of talk about pollution—air pollution, water pollution—which has become a fashionable slogan. Politicians like to raise a smokescreen by using this slogan to conceal certain more "real" problems.

Personally I have the impression that one of the worst sorts of pollution threatening us is what I call "information pollution." By that I mean (and the concluding remarks of the preceding paragraph alluded to it) that we are in the process of piling up an enormous quantity of unrelated data, in a disorderly fashion, and in such abundance that it is becoming almost impossible to unscramble it. Naturally this "information heap" is both redundant and contradictory (most of it being garbage) and because of the quantity alone it is impossible to get to its usable part. Information pollution also means that the "waste products" of our present knowledge are polluting the usable part of that knowledge.

Let us consider an information system of n elements (transmitting and receiving stations, messages, or anything else that can be meant by "element"). The highest degree of potential connection between the n elements will be represented by the complete graph Kn, which assumes that all the elements are *directly* linked to each other. Such a graph runs the risk of being very complicated, but the itineraries linking one element to any other will be, in this case, the simplest possible. The only difficulty with this schema lies in the fact that the graph generates $CKn = k \cdot n^4$ crossovers, which can all be considered sources of potential conflict (points at which errors originate or where a particular signal is necessary to eliminate such errors). In an organization based on information disseminated through communications from the outside, this implies that the field of possible errors is proportional as a fourth power to the amount of useful information. Such a proportion represents totally inadequate efficiency.

The implications of this fact doubtless suggest why we are presently witnessing a process of self-destruction in political entities of large dimensions, with more than 200 million inhabitants, (such as the U. S. A. and the U. S. S. R.). There seems to be a kind of natural threshold, analogous to "critical mass" in nuclear physics (conflicts become explosive beyond a certain determined number of elements composing a mass).

Let us imagine an organization not based on information coming from outside and then channeled, but where the necessary information is contained in a "band"—a memory set up in advance, a kind of a priori knowledge. This organization would be able to function without producing the great number of potential conflicts which we spoke about earlier, but, on the other hand, it would become relatively rigid and impossible to "readjust."

Let us now try to examine society considered as a group of individuals possessing certain common characteristics. Either the characteristics will be acknowledged as common by the members of that society—in which case it will be a society of the "immediate communication" type (for if these characteristics are lacking, the members of that society will no longer recognize each other) or these common characteristics will be observed by someone outside the society—and it will then be considered a "memory" type of society (in which case, the outside observer can very easily detect similarities—dictated by a memory of the a priori type—which remain unknown to the members of the society itself). I am using the terms "society of the immediate communication type" and "society of the memory type" just as labels, whose meaning will be indicated later.

Let us try to imagine, by way of example, a science fiction scenario showing diverse organizations in the form of societies belonging to worlds other than ours. We shall try to describe these societies by deducing their characteristics from a certain number of supposed "fundamental traits."

7.2.1 A TELEPATHIC SOCIETY
Let us imagine a society where direct, immediate mental transmission exists among the members. Thus all the members of that society could pick up all the thoughts of the others, whether or not they wanted to.

Obviously, such a society would not have a language, since any exchange of information in code would be superfluous: that would also be true for art, science, and so on. Even acts provoking pleasure or displeasure could not be carried out by a limited number of members of that society, without their being felt at the same time by all the other members.

Another consequence: that society could have only a collective memory, with no individual memory or consciousness of self in any of its members. No isolated event could be recorded so as to permit its later identification by its effects since all the members of the society would have recorded it at the same time, and therefore no system to detect regularities could be constructed. Among other concepts, this society would not have that of time, for, since its collective memory would be incapable of distinguishing an ordered sequence of certain nonlocalizable events (for example, the case of a succession of events affecting only one member of the society at a time, and affecting them one after the other, could not be detected, for the collective memory would not know if an event had affected the same member n times, or n different members a single time).

Such a society would thus be almost entirely cut off from our mode of thought, and it could not understand any structure we use.

7.2.2 A "MASS-SENSITIVE" SOCIETY

This time, let us imagine the existence of a society of beings insensitive to light waves, sound waves, or any other kind of waves, in other words, to all "media" (of information) reflected by surfaces. However, these beings would react to variations in mass, potential, and so on, and would be capable of localizing them. Naturally the members of such a society would never see a surface or a form (just as a scale is not sensitive to the form, but to the mass of the objects placed on its platform) but they would "see" the slightest variation in mass, or in the configuration of potentials.

This society would also be "telepathic," in the sense that it would register the totality or the largest part of the mental processes of all its members, as well as all the physical processes, within a certain distance, and simultaneously.

This society would thus have an organization analogous to that of the telepathic society.

7.2.3 A SOCIETY OF LEMMINGS

To conclude, let us imagine beings who simply have no memory whatsoever. Naturally, these beings could not survive, since they could not learn how to anticipate dangerous external influences, and would be rapidly exterminated en masse by communal accidents such as falling from a precipice one after the other.

For these beings, the sole chance of survival would lie in direct, immediate communication among all of them: pain, acting upon one of them at the moment of the accident, would thus stop all the others at that same moment, and before the pain disappeared would prevent them from repeating the act carried out by the one already affected by the pain. Although immediately forgotten after the accident, this telepathic warning could nevertheless preserve the society from extinction, provided that the number of its members was sufficiently large so that even an accident of long duration could not do away with these "lemmings" one by one.

SOME SUPERFICIAL CONCLUSIONS

Although they begin from different definitions, the three examples cited are in fact one and the same case: all three describe an organization in which the paired operations "communication/memory" function differently from the way they do in our society.

Now our society in its present form possesses a very well-developed memory and a woefully weak communication system. It therefore functions by means of "structures," or systems of abbreviation which alleviate this deficiency somewhat.

In contrast, the imaginary societies that I have described have no formal memory; but they compensate for this lack by a system of immediate communication. Without such a system (as in the case of the "lemmings") they could not survive.

There is not much exchange possible between societies based on pure memory and societies based on pure communication: for the latter, our "structures" have no meaning.

In these terms, the noncompetitive society of which I spoke at the beginning of this chapter would be a society based principally on memory,* far more than our present society is.

I am now going to try to estimate the chances that such a society will come to exist in the future.

On the practical level, until now we have considered organizations of the "most connected" type (based on communication) and the "least connected" type (based on memory). We discovered that the tendency toward a "more connected" society, based on communication, led very quickly and inevitably to information pollution, and that the tendency toward a "less connected" society, based on memory, implied the necessity of a preestablished a priori memory content. Now, one could not imagine that such a memory content could be established without the existence of an earlier organization based on communication.

Such thoughts can have rather comic consequences: each of these organizations (societies), which are mutually complementary, *constitutes a deadly "virus" for the other.* (I call a "viral effect" the destructive influence of an external structural rule which contradicts and breaks down the existing structural rules in a system represented by a network, in such a way that most of the operations that could be carried out on the original network can be no longer once the "viral effect" has been introduced.)

Thus the noncompetitive society, based on memory, which is in fact a nonsociety, would necessarily be an agent of destruction in our present society, which is based principally on communication and a prey to information pollution. At any rate this society does in fact react with instinctive hatred against "hippies," who are the precursors of a noncompetitive society.

(We can observe a simplified example of a case of viral effect, when a traffic network planned for a specific type of organization proves unsuitable for another type of organization.) These observations allow us to give a new definition of infrastructure (defined in another chapter) as the network that best resists viruses.

*The noncompetitive society is, in fact, a tendency to promote noncommunication (as I have said, it is a nonsociety).

In my predictions I dare to assume that the noncompetitive society will destroy ours. It may be that by the time it becomes the predominant model, the remains of our society will in turn have the same viral effect and produce the opposite tendency, and so on.

The question that presents itself is this: can this alternating development be considered a Markovian process leading to a stable state?

To suggest a reply to this question, I must turn to explanations of a general order: if I begin to construct (map) the representation of a set of individuals connected in a certain way (that is, in a society, as we have defined it), with the individuals represented by points and their relationships by lines, I shall necessarily obtain graphs or networks. Earlier I called the "private city" of an individual the figure constituted by the point corresponding to that individual and by all the other points connected to him by a single arc. The "mapping" of a society will thus be the "interconnected" set of these private cities, and it will necessarily contain a certain number of crossovers (potential conflicts). These networks representing a society probably include repetitions, and therefore "regularities," that is to say, a "structure." What can we know about that structure?

There is—sad to say—only one human institution whose structure (in the sense meant here) is well known, and that is the army (probably the stablest of all structured human organizations ever invented). The graph of an army is a "tree" of fourth degree, based on the empirical observation that a man who commands cannot give an order and supervise its execution by more than three persons at a time.

This implies that the structural rules, and consequently the weakness or strength of an army organization, are easy to recognize: we are dealing with a familiar structure. (It is interesting to note that new nations generally begin their existence by organizing their armies.)

As for the form that structural rules for the mapping of societies may take, based on the concept of the "private city," I can suggest several possibilities. We may ask ourselves the following questions:
a. What is the smallest closed circuit? (That is, what number of persons can constitute the smallest "group?")
b. What is the classification of the degrees for a point in this mapping?

THE STRUCTURAL DIFFERENCES
BETWEEN THE PRIVATE CITY CONCEPT
AND HIERARCHICAL ORGANIZATION
BRING UP AN IMPORTANT QUESTION
ABOUT THE SOCIETY OF THE FUTURE

PRIVATE CITIES   MILITARY ORGANIZATION

WHAT ARE THE   HERE, THE STRUCTURAL RULES
STRUCTURAL RULES?   ARE ALREADY KNOWN:
THEY ARE STILL
UNEXPLORED   A TREE OF DEGREE 4.

                                  INTERPRETATION:
                                  RAPID DISSEMINATION OF INFOR-
                                  MATION IN THE GROUP;
                                  FRAGILITY.

Figure 60

(That is, how many persons can be in contact with a central individual?)
c. What is the most symmetrical figure for such a graph? (In other words,
what is the simplest legislative code for the group in which there are the
fewest conflicts?) And so on.

It is by trying to answer these questions (something which has never
been done anywhere, as far as I know) that we might discover several
of the fundamental properties of societies.

Thanks to this research, we might also discover what laws concerning
"thresholds" govern societies based on communication and societies
based on memory.

When these regularities and other analogous ones become known to
us, it will be easier to settle the question of the Markovian or non-
Markovian nature of a sequence of events that transforms a social organization of a certain type into one of a different type. To translate
the question into other terms: does the "mapping" of a society allow

for an underlying cycle of different states of that society or not? Of course, I do not think that the solution is that simple, but I use this hypothesis simply to show what type of answer I hope to obtain through these investigations.

  As long as these questions, and others of the same kind, are not answered one way or the other (through the discovery of regularities or of their absence), I believe that present operational methods cannot lead us very far, and that they will never be "trustworthy" (likely to yield certainties). A typical example is "game theory," the application of which to our subject will always be fallacious, since the process we are studying may very well be cyclical, and since it is therefore impossible to see how this theory, which considers how well strategies bring the game to its conclusion (win or tie) could be applied to it.

  To "conclude this conclusion" I should like to return to the concept of democratization; that is to say, direct decision regarding operations by all the persons concerned who stand to lose *because* of these opera-

THE STRUCTURAL RULES
FOR A GRAPH REPRESENTING
A NETWORK OF PRIVATE CITIES
COULD BE OF THE KIND:

1) N-CIRCUITS BASED ON
   A GIVEN POINTS

2) CIRCUITS CONTAINING m
   CROSSOVERS

3) N-CIRCUITS CONTAINING m
   CROSSOVERS

4) k CROSSOVERS CONTAINED
   IN TREES STARTING FROM
   POINTS OF DEGREE ∝

ETC

Figure 61

INTERPRETATIONS OF SUBGRAPHS
CONTAINED IN A NETWORK:

 TREE OF DEGREE 0 : HIERARCHICAL ORGANIZATION

RAPID DISSEMINATION
GREAT VULNERABILITY
NO CONFLICT
UNCHANGEABILITY

 N- CIRCUIT : EGALITARIAN ORGANIZATION

NO CENTER
SEMI STABILITY
NO CONFLICT
UNCHANGEABILITY

 SATURATED N-GRAPH : IDEAL ORGANIZATION

MOST STABLE ORGANIZATION WITH NO CONFLICTS
PRIVILEGED SUBGROUPS
ADMITS CYCLES OF REORGANIZATION

 COMPLETE N·GRAPH : EXPLOSIVE UTOPIA

MOST STABILITY
MAXIMUM CONFLICTS
PERMITS ANY CHANGE

Figure 62

tions. Democracy, in this sense, is an institution based on memory and
not based on communication, since in order to be capable of making a
decision individuals must have a "memory content" established a priori
(this a priori memory content includes, for example, concepts of personal interest, self-defense, and so on). In reality, all higher animals live
in a democracy based on memory; we usually call their memory content "instinct."

If we wish to fight for a more democratic social organization, we
must use communication in its present state as if it were a tool destined
to obsolesce, whose principal use is the creation and establishment of
"memory contents." This means that popularization and instruction
are the most important activities.

The "Flatwriter," a tool which is based on memory and eliminates
information "breakdown," is a good example of how this new society
could be achieved.

One last question remains: do we really want this other society or
not? But that is an emotional question and I can answer it only with

reference to myself. The only purpose of my proposition is to demonstrate how far "objective" thought can lead us, avoiding the error common to most predictions, in which thought mistakes its own desires for reality.

APPENDIX (1972) SOCIETY ⇌ ENVIRONMENT

A.1 TERMINOLOGY

A.1.1 SOCIETY CAN BE MAPPED BY A GRAPH

I call "society" a set of individuals in which there exists some sort of "relation" between any two individuals belonging to the set. A person who has no such "relation" to at least one other who in his turn is related to the others, can be considered a person "out of society."

Let us suppose that I would like to sketch the image of a society. I will first draw all persons belonging to it, then continue by drawing lines linking any two persons between whom I observe an existing relation. I will thus represent this society by means of a figure in which any one person will be linked to any other by at least one "path" passing from one to the other by the intermediary of other persons.

If I replace the "mannikins" of this map of the society by points, the result will be a figure consisting of points and lines, in which there is at least one path between any pair of points chosen arbitrarily ("connected graph").

Obviously this graph gives an oversimplified image of a society. Using this figure will require further explanation.

I will thus reexamine the concept of "relations," which I represented by lines in the figure. First I will try to find out who drew it. Otherwise stated, one has to know *who* the observer of this society is.

I should point out immediately that different observers will see different "maps" for the same society. In most cases it will be difficult to find two observers who would attribute the same importance to the same relation; thus the "importance" of relations cannot be observed without error, and therefore I will not introduce "importance" into my terminology.

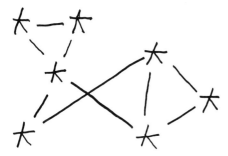

Figure 1

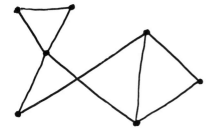

Figure 2

On the other hand, the mere existence of a direct relation between two individuals belonging to a society can be observed. This means that the existence or the nonexistence of a "line" in a graph representing a society can be agreed on by a large number of potential observers. I will thus be content to *note* the existence of a relation.

Another characteristic of such "relations" can be observed and noted: their "direction." Let me explain the term.

In observing two persons who "communicate" (and thus a relation between them) we can generally state that once the communication is finished, the one or the other (or both) of the two persons changes his previous behavior. We will say, in such a case, that one of the two persons (or both of them) received an "influence" from the other one. This influence has a "direction," which points from the person who exerts the influence to the other one who receives it.

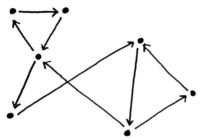

Figure 3

I will define "influence" as a relation between two individuals which has an observable direction.

In conclusion, a society will thus be represented by a direct connected graph, that is, by a figure consisting of points and lines, in which there is no point not linked by at least one path to any other point (when arrow directions are not considered) and in which every line carries an arrow representing the direction of the influence in this particular link.

A.1.2 STRUCTURAL CHARACTERISTICS OF SOCIETIES

This representation of a society makes it possible to describe its structural characteristics by using maps constructed with graphs as explained earlier. These characteristics do not refer to any measurable size, as I had to exclude, first of all, the possibility of knowing importance, intensities, and so on, of "influences" in general. I have thus limited myself to considering certain topological properties of these graphs, in order to characterize social organizations. These topological properties indicate characteristics implied by the linkage schemes, the paths, and the circuits within such maps of a society; they correspond to those of the influences within a set of individuals.

To get to the description of such important characteristics I shall invoke an image: the image of the "situation" of a particular person within a society. This "social situation" will be defined by influences this particular person *receives from* and *exerts upon* the other members of the society. For example, if he exerts an influence upon four of his neighbors and he does not receive any influence from anybody, he could be considered as having more "power" than another person who also exerts four influences but receives two influences from others.

Thus "social situation" of a particular person will be expressed by the difference of the sum of influences starting with him and of the sum of influences having him as their endpoint.

In practice, the social situation of a particular person corresponds to his balance of influences. But—and this is important—we calculate this balance without associating any "size" difference with different arrows, as we have agreed that "size" of influence is not observable.

We will thus consider, to make an inevitable simplification, any influence exerted by one person on another one, as having the same importance when observed by anybody not related to any of these two persons (that is, by an observer not belonging to the same society).

This convention does not mean, obviously, that the two persons linked by this influence do not attribute to it any value, any importance whatever.

We can be sure that they do, and even that very probably this importance will be different for each of the two: the one who exerts the influence might consider it as being important, and the other, who receives it, might ignore it; or inversely, one might ignore the influence he exerts on others and the ones who receive it might appreciate its importance.

To avoid such ambiguity I had to take as a standard the observation of someone exterior to the society observed. But if this observer considers all direct influences as equal, he might observe a degradation of "indirect" influences (influences transmitted by several intermediary persons), degradation through errors, omissions, because of successive transmissions (degradation resulting from what information theory calls "noise").

We will use, in order to describe this degradation of an indirect influence because of the necessary transmissions, a simple rule: we will suppose that the "intensity" of an influence will decay in inverse proportion to the number of intermediary transmissions necessary to its forwarding.

We are now ready to define the "social situation" of any person within a society by an observer exterior to this society. It will be expressed by the difference of the sum of all influences (direct and indirect) exerted

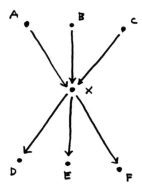

Figure 4

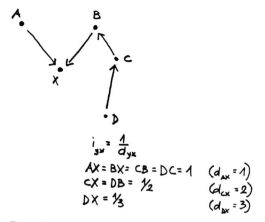

$$i_{yx} = \frac{1}{d_{yx}}$$

$AX = BX = CB = DC = 1 \quad (d_{AX} = 1)$

$CX = DB = \tfrac{1}{2} \qquad\quad (d_{CX} = 2)$

$DX = \tfrac{1}{3} \qquad\qquad (d_{DX} = 3)$

Figure 5

by this particular person upon all other persons within the society, and of the sum of all influences starting from all other persons in the society and received by him.

In order to do this simple calculation it is sufficient to construct the "path matrix" of the graph mapping the society in question. On the basis of this graph (or of this matrix) we can find both sums necessary to define the parameter of "social situation."

Using this method, we can obtain not only the social situation of any person within the society of our example (here containing 7 persons) that we obtained, but also the real "hierarchy" established (frequently in a tacit way) within the society. Obviously, the hierarchy we find in the figure is only the "hierarchy" observable by somebody *exterior* to this society. It is quite possible that the "hierarchy" as observed by Mr. A. or by Mr. B. differs sensibly from the "objective hierarchy."

Let us suppose, now, that one member of this society decides to leave it for some reason of his own. Immediately the "hierarchy" will be transformed as a consequence of his leaving it. Certain persons remaining within the society will benefit from this defection (their "social situation" will be improved); others will be prejudiced. Thus, if we suppose—in order to keep the example simple—that all members of the society want to get a "higher" place in the hierarchy, those who benefit by the defection of Mr. X can be considered his "adversaries," who are interested in removing him from the society. On the contrary, those who are prejudiced by the departure of Mr. X. will try to keep him: they are his "allies."

Using a simple function, which I call that of "dependence" of a particular person in the society upon the departure of Mr. X., we can construct a "table of alliances" characteristic of this society.

"Dependence" can be calculated in a simple way: by obtaining the difference between the social situations of a person belonging to the society before and after the departure of Mr. X. The first social situation can be calculated on the graph which maps the society as a whole (Mr. X. included); the second social situation will be obtained by calculating on a subgraph of the same graph, the subgraph not containing Mr. X.

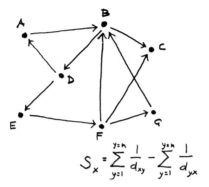

$$S_x = \sum_{y=1}^{y=n} \frac{1}{d_{xy}} - \sum_{y=1}^{y=n} \frac{1}{d_{yx}}$$

Figure 6

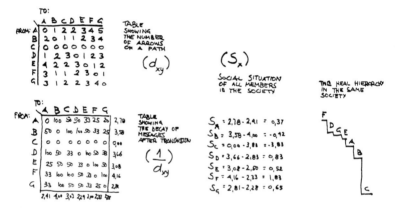

Figure 7

$$D_{x(z)} = S_x - S_x(y \neq z) = \left(\sum_{y=1}^{y=h} \frac{1}{d_{xy}} - \sum_{y=1}^{y=h} \frac{1}{d_{yx}} \right) - \left(\sum_{y=1}^{y=h} \frac{1}{d_{xy}} - \sum_{y=1}^{y=h} \frac{1}{d_{yx}} \text{ and } y \neq z \right)$$

FOES	MrX	ALLIES
BCDE	A	FG
ACDEG	B	F
	C	ABDEFG
ACE	D	BG
CDEG	E	AB
ABCG	F	E
ABCDF	G	E

Figure 8

ALLIES:
THOSE WHO WANT
TO KEEP MR X
WITHIN THE SOCIETY

FOES:
THOSE WHO WANT
TO CHASE MR X
FROM THE SOCIETY

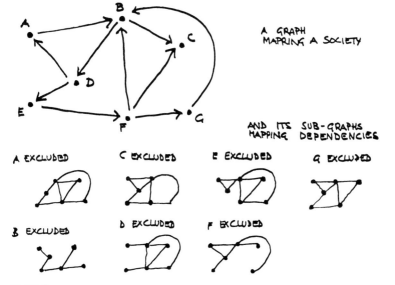

A GRAPH
MAPPING A SOCIETY

AND ITS SUB-GRAPHS
MAPPING DEPENDENCIES

A EXCLUDED   C EXCLUDED   E EXCLUDED   G EXCLUDED

B EXCLUDED   D EXCLUDED   F EXCLUDED

Figure 9

We obtained thus, by a method sufficiently simple to be used by a ten-year-old child, a fairly good description of the real structure of a society. This method can be used for any society imaginable.

A.1.3 "EGALITARIAN" AND "HIERARCHIC" SOCIETY

I will try to define, after all these preliminary explanations, two concepts of society, concepts which I consider important: "egalitarian" society and "hierarchic" society.

I call a society "egalitarian" if all its members have the same social situation. Put otherwise, in an egalitarian society the difference of the totality of influences exerted and of the totality of influences received will be the *same* for everybody. Such a society thus contains no "upper class" influencing the others.

An egalitarian society is thus a possible one. There are a large number of graphs which satisfy this condition (even though certain constraints restrict this number, constraints we will investigate later on).

Another type of society having great importance because it is a very common one, is "hierarchic": this type of society can be represented by a "tree" (a graph in which between any pair of points there is but one path). This society is characterized by a "degressive" hierarchy of social situation, starting from the "apex" (i.e., the person represented by the apex is the most powerful, the persons just below him are somewhat less powerful, and so on). Its other characteristic is a "progressive" hierarchy of alliances, progression starting from the same apex. Thus "dependence," or change in social situation caused by the departure of

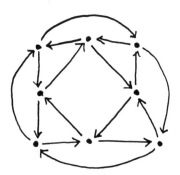

Figure 10

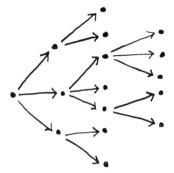

Figure 11

somebody from the society, will be less noticeable for persons at the "bottom" of the society than at its "top."

We saw before that this method of representing a society is based on the exchange of influence within a set of individuals. The two types of society sketched above are practically two schemes of exchange diametrically opposed. In egalitarian society exchange can start with any member of the society and will with certainty reach all other members, perhaps slowly, but surely. On the other hand, in hierarchic society, there is but one person who can start an influence which will reach all members of the society, and it will do so relatively quickly. As for the probability that this influence will reach everyone, it is very low (because the noncooperation of only one person somewhere in the society represents a locus for a certain number of paths).

Obviously enough, these two types of society are not the only ones possible: I picked them because they are particularly important. As a matter of fact, all social utopias have as a goal an egalitarian society, and all technical organizations are based on hierarchic society. Evidently, neither is a perfect model, but there are many organizations tending toward the one or the other of these models.

A.1.4 SOCIETY CONTAINS BOTH PEOPLE AND OBJECTS

I would like to correct a simplification I had to make (among others) when I began this paper. I defined society as a set of individuals in which there exists some sort of relation (influence) between any two individuals. In reality, we are related not only to men by a system of influences, but also to objects.

I will be thus obliged to introduce a new definition for society, as being a set of persons and objects linked by a system of influences. Thus a society can be considered as a mixed mechanism containing men and objects.

In order to be more precise, I have to state what I consider the criterion of difference between human beings and objects, from the point of view of this study. This difference results from the fact that men are conscious of their situation in society, as opposed to objects, which do not care.

This definition makes it possible for us to imagine other social alternatives, which could be realized more easily than most social utopias (even if these alternatives are submitted to the constraints I will talk about later). One such alternative would be a society egalitarian for human beings but hierarchic for the objects belonging to it.

A.1.5 SOCIETY AND ENVIRONMENT ARE SYNONYMS

The first important result we get by applying our new terminology (that of the definition of society and its mapping by graphs) will be the equivalence of society and environment.

This equivalence is expressed in the definition "set of persons and objects." Indeed, the definition generally used for environment, "the set of objects influenced by and influencing men," is inadequate. Why not "objects *and* persons"? As for the definition of society, it was discussed in the preceding paragraph.

"Society" and "environment" are thus the same set. My own term for this set is "others." This term is really the most accurate, because it refers to the person who uses it. Thus, if Mr. X. is talking about society or about his environment and he uses the term "the others" he includes Mr. Y., his house, and so on, but will not include himself. On the other hand, if Mr. Y. uses the same term, he will include Mr. X., a tree, and so on, and the whole system he is linked to, except himself.

"The others" are others for every one of us.

A.2 CRITICAL GROUP

A.2.1 "VALENCE" AND DEGRADATION OF INFLUENCE

After this long section about terminology we are still far from the conclusion of this study. We have still to make clear ceratin basic concepts, but happily, we have the most difficult ones behind us.

The first concept to be investigated is the one I call "valence": it signifies a property, observable and biologically determined, belonging to the human animal. This property defines how many centers of interest can occupy simultaneously the attention of man. For example, I can read two books simultaneously (even if with some difficulty), perhaps even three; but, surely, I could never understand ten different books at the same time. In this case my valence will be perhaps three, perhaps more, but by no means as much as ten.

"Valence" will thus limit the number of persons who can influence (or who can be influenced by) one member of a society during a given period of reference. Valence will be visualized in the map of a society (or of an environment) by the "degree" of a given point corresponding to a person (we call "degree" the number of lines incident to a given point).

The second key concept, that is, the degradation of an influence by successive transmissions, was mentioned earlier, when I discussed the way to calculate real hierarchy (social situation) within a society.

Degradation of influence through successive transmissions also implies an observable and biologically determined property of the human animal: indeed, this degradation depends on our mental capacity. I call the "channel capacity" of a particular person (or of a species) the capacity for transmitting a message with a number of errors, where this number is characteristic of the "channel capacity" of this person (or species or sort of object).

This property is a very limiting one for a society: it implies that an indirect influence submitted to more intermediary transmissions than admitted by the "channel capacity" will decay completely: it will be indistinguishable beyond a given number of transmissions.

"Valence" and "channel capacity" of the human animal represent two natural thresholds *which cannot be crossed* without great difficulty. These two thresholds affect the rhythm of exchange of influences among human beings (and objects), thus within social organizations (or environments) which in the end are dependent on the numerical value of these thresholds.

A.2.2 THRESHOLD VALUES

The possibility of practical application of these two thresholds (valence and channel capacity) for societies or environments comes from the fact that these thresholds determine the numerical size (quantity) of "elements" (men and objects) that can belong to a society without having a disturbing effect on its functioning. Implicitly, the same thresholds determine the number of links within a society. Thus, for example, it would be impossible to realize an "egalitarian" society containing n' humans, m' objects and w' links if the respective thresholds do not admit more than n' humans, m' objects, and w' links, and when $n, m,$ and w are respectively smaller than $n', m',$ and w'.

It would be just as impossible to conceive of a "hierarchic" society containing n'' humans, m'' objects and w'' links if the specific thresholds imply numbers less for both "elements" and "links" for a "hierarchic" society. Expressed simply, a society or an environment having a determined structure (in the sense used in the first section) cannot contain more elements and links than admitted by certain established threshold values.

We will call "critical groups" the largest set of elements (humans, objects and links) for which the functioning of a group, characterized by a determined structure, still can be assured.

The concept of the "critical group" is perhaps the most important re-

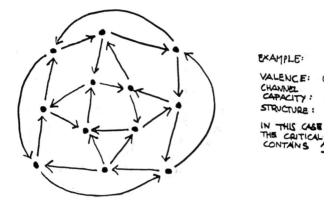

EXAMPLE:

VALENCE: $v = 4$
CHANNEL CAPACITY: $c = 5$
STRUCTURE: EGALITARIAN

IN THIS CASE THE CRITICAL GROUP CONTAINS 12 PERSONS

Figure 12

sult of this study because a comparison of any organization with the "critical group" corresponding to its structural category shows immediately whether this organization is realizable or not. Most utopias or projects fail less because of the impossibility of implementing the ideas on which they are based than because they exceed the size admitted by the "critical group." Very often it is exactly the success of a group's ideology that is the tool of its self-destruction, for this success promotes the group's expansion and when expansion passes the critical group size, the group "explodes."

A.2.3 "CRITICAL GROUP SIZE" AS A SPECIES CHARACTERISTIC

"Critical group" is a result of two biological factors (valence and channel capacity) and one topological factor (the structure of a society). Its size is thus independent of any ideology, technique, or knowledge; otherwise expressed, of any "artificial" factor invented by man. The three decisive factors depend thus on "natural laws," and the rule of the "critical group" is itself a "natural law."

Two of these factors (valence and channel capacity) are biological factors: thus they differ with every species. The third factor is invariable in the sense that it is the same for any species.

Thus, "critical group size" varies with every species: it is different for men, for monkeys, lions, herrings, or bees. But for any species, it can be *known*, and the numerical size of the critical group could be considered as a *species characteristic.*

If we consider, for example, an animal species, let us say, elephants, we will find that a herd of elephants varies as to the number of individuals belonging to it, but that this herd never exceeds a given number: that of the critical group size of elephants.

Alienation of man could thus be a consequence of enormously exceeding human critical group size: we live with more people than we can tolerate, and with more objects than we can rely on, and all this without becoming biologically a different species.

Exceeding critical group size puts an overload on the brain of an individual, an overload which he cannot bear.

A.3 CRITICAL GROUP AND ENVIRONMENT

A.3.1 THE OVERPRODUCTION OF WASTE

Statements concerning the critical group for living beings (men and animals) have their analogues for objects, but I will reserve my interest for the real world, which contains both living beings and objects.

I have said already that environment means "the others." We are not necessarily in contact with all others, living beings or objects; thus it is more accurate to reserve the expression "the others" for those with whom we are linked in an observable manner.

"Environmental crisis" results from improvements in our manner of observation: today there are many known relations which were before nonobservable. Many other relations, which could have been observable, were not observed because they did not attract our attention.

One such relation, a very important one, concerns production of waste. Any living organism, or any organization containing living beings, functions through selection of components useful for its survival. The proportion of useful components to all components in an environment is very small; thus the organisms or organizations mentioned reject a quantity of components which is far greater than the quantity retained. A living being is thus a "waste factory."

If waste is "recyclable," it is not in any amount. If it is produced in an amount above a determinable threshold, pollution (accumulation of waste) begins. It is a question of a critical amount of waste, this amount being determined by the structure of the organism or organization which makes the selection of useful components and thus produces waste, and by its relation to "other" organisms or organizations.

The key to avoiding overproduction of waste is thus the operation of selecting what is useful. Today, with our way of practicing selection, the principal production of humanity is waste: about 70 percent of human energy is invested in it.

A.3.2 "RUBBISH IS BEAUTIFUL," OR ADAPTATION TO MAKE WASTE USEFUL

As the preceding paragraph points out, waste is waste because it was considered useless during the process of selection, very often for arbitrary reasons. We could reduce overproduction of waste by a simple method: by changing the use criteria for certain objects, thus changing the process of selection.

To explain this idea, I will use a historical (or even "prehistorical") example. I have in mind the "heroic" period of the agricultural revolution.

The first thing the farmer did was to cut down and tear out native vegetation from the land he wanted to sow; then from season to season he threw away stones that he found on his land. The product of this deforestation and of this disposal of stones was genuine rubbish to the farmer: wood and stones. One of the first inventions of the primitive farmer was the "recycling" of this rubbish in the form of using it to construct his shelters.

This recycling did not imply any material transformation of the rubbish, not even any intervention of some new technology: it consisted only of a change in man's attitude toward some waste which began to accumulate in quantities over the critical amount.

Prehistoric man thus avoided one kind of pollution by nothing more complicated than changing his own attitude.

Let us imagine, as a second example. a similar change of attitude for today: I planned several years ago to propose an international competition under the title "rubbish is beautiful." The basic idea was inspired by the fact that many of today's artistic movements use rubbish for works of art. So why not try to transfer heaps of rubbish into monumental art, monuments for our time? A large part of rubbish is not biodegradable, and much effort is required to dispose of it, outside the course of everyday life. Why should we dispose of it? Why should we not use it for the construction of "megasculptures," collective ones if possible? Let us imagine, for example, a pyramid of plastic bottles, or a large sculpture made of wrecked cars.

The conclusion is that being faced with pollution (that is, we exceed the critical amount of rubbish) it would be easier to change our attitude toward waste than to stop waste.

Expressed otherwise, a critical amount of useless components is characteristic of a "species of objects" (exactly as critical group size was for a living species), and of the organization men impose on these objects. It is easier to change this organization than the characteristics of the species, once waste exceeds the critical amount.

A.3.3 "CRITICAL GROUP" FOR PRODUCTION

Let us try to correlate the two kinds of thresholds:

1. The critical group size of a living species depends on the "valence" and "channel capacity" of this species, and of the structure of the group ("structure" in its topological meaning).

2. The critical amount of waste depends on the human group organization, on its attitude toward waste and on the properties of the transformation process (selection of useful components).

Although all factors of the critical group are independent of human will, factors of the critical amount for objects are largely dependent on human desires.

It is interesting to remark that the critical amount of rubbish is partly a function of the critical group of the human species, and partly of the transformation process producing a specific object.

This remark opens the question whether a return to social groups with fewer members than the "critical group" would not resolve pollution problems, at least in a large number of cases. Would not such a return to social groups smaller than the critical group also reduce communication between groups, and thus commerce (the most ancient type of communication) and overproduction (production of goods for other use than one's own)?

I do not pretend to be able to answer these questions; the only answer I can give is that they seem to me very important ones. But there is one thing I am sure of: a return to groups smaller than the critical one would resolve a great many of today's economic problems: relations between production, property, and exchange. (I shall develop these ideas in more detail).

In the following sections I discuss some social organizations and analyze them according to the points considered in the first three sections.

A.4 REALIZABLE UTOPIAS

A.4.1 THE "NONPATERNALIST" SCHEME

I have investigated up to this point the "objective" elements of this study: definitions, a terminology based on graphs (thus on mathema-

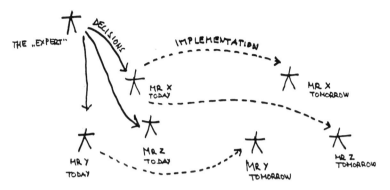

Figure 13

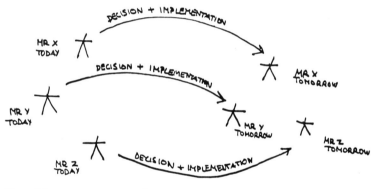

Figure 14

tics), critical groups (a concept belonging both to biology and to mathematics) characteristic of man and environment. I have made no moral judgments, and I have mentioned examples only as illustration, without committing myself by saying whether I consider these examples desirable or not.

Now I will change my approach, and I will talk about schemes and organizations and state my opinion about them. Thus I plan to make moral judgments, and I will use statements from the three preceding sections for reference, to be as precise as I can be in this condensed study.

I will start by explaining what I call "paternalist" and "nonpaternalist" schemes.

I call "paternalist" any organization in which one or more persons make decisions, decisions which are supposed to be implemented by other persons who have to take all risks involved in the decisions, without any risk to the persons who made them. Obviously enough, I don't want to suggest that the decision makers, who reach their decisions at the expense of "others," do so by bad intentions. In this category belong all sorts of "experts": people who pretend to know better, what to do for the well-being of others, than the "others" themselves.

I call "nonpaternalist" any organization in which all decisions are made by the persons who implement them and who take the whole risk implied by the decisions, and where there exist no "others" who risk getting the "fallout" from the decisions.

I personally think that the nonpaternalist scheme is desirable, and that the paternalist scheme is dangerous, inefficient, and unjust. My judgment that it is dangerous and inefficient is an "objective" judgment (it can be explained in general terms comprehensible to anybody), but my judgment about its injustice is a moral judgment.

A.4.2 "OBJECTIVE LANGUAGE" IS A CONDITION SINE QUA NON FOR NONPATERNALIST SCHEMES

The nonpaternalist scheme is realizable only if any individual involved in a process is informed about the following points:

1. The possibilities he can choose from in making his decision ("repertoire")

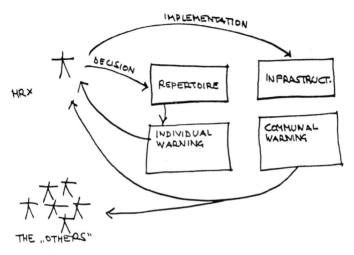

Figure 15

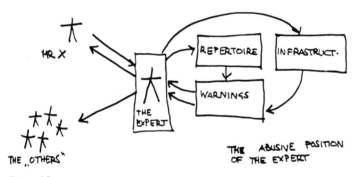

Figure 16

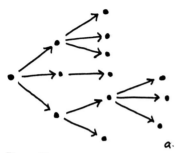

a.

Figure 17

2. The consequences for him personally; what he can expect from his decision (warning about consequences to the individual)

3. The rules of the context wherein he will implement his decision ("infrastructure")

4. The consequences of his decision for others (warning about consequences for the community).

Conditions necessary for such information cannot be assured unless an "objective terminology," a "code," is used. (Thus, the section of this appendix devoted to terminology is the guarantee that this is a "nonpaternalist" study.)

This is a necessary condition because without an objective terminology neither the "repertoire" nor the "warnings" nor the "infrastructure" can be described without imprecision; and genuine decisions cannot be made without knowing these elements. If a particular person does not know them, he can be taken advantage of by some "expert" who tries to impose upon him his own decisions; for someone not knowing such a terminology, the expert will become a self-appointed "translator" who might use the "others'" ignorance.

The "repertoire" of social organizations (obviously oversimplified) will include the following:

1. Hierarchical society, represented by a "tree" (a graph in which there is but one path between any two points).

2. Egalitarian society, represented by a strongly connected, well-oriented graph (a graph in which there are several paths between any pair of points and in which arrow directions are ordered so that any region is

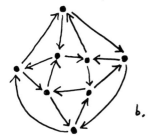

Figure 18

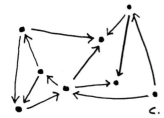

Figure 19

limited by a closed circuit, with the same arrow direction.

3. "Undetermined" society, represented by a connected, directed graph without supplementary conditions.

Consequences of the choice of one organization, whether they concern the individual or the community, can be foreseen by the simple formulas discussed in the section on social situation: warnings will thus describe both hierarchies and alliances within a particular social organization.

Evidently, my hyopthesis in the first sections requires that the terminology describe equally well a society or an environment.

Thus we are prepared to implement nonpaternalist schemes.

A.4.3 SOME REALIZABLE EXAMPLES OF EGALITARIAN SOCIETY

Personally, and for moral reasons, I am for egalitarian society, and I will devote this subsection to its realizability. I would like to enumerate some examples which can be carried out following the nonpaternalist scheme.

1. The "noncompetitive" society

We are often victims of a superstition which interprets competition as an imperative of the survival instinct. Competition might be a means to assure survival of the fittest if it is directed at scarce commodities (like, for example, food in an arid region).

Once all means of survival (food, water, air, shelter, available space, and so on) are abundant (naturally or artificially), competition for survival is no longer necessary. We (humans) invent, then, a "fictive scarcity," a "privilege" (material or immaterial) which can be assured only in limited quantities. Such a privilege (scarce by definition) becomes the "premium" inciting to competition. All societies today are based on an internal struggle for privileges (luxury, status, and so on) which are not directly necessary for survival.

Let us imagine a society which would renounce these privileges. It would be in essence egalitarian, and it could be realized only if the number of its elements (persons and objects) did not exceed the limit imposed by the critical group.

2. The "anonymous" society

We all like to "sign" things we make: shoes, works of art, omelets, or poems. Is it true that a shoe, a work of art, an omelet, or a poem makes me happier if I know who made it?

The persons-objects relation is organized in two "path sections": (a) from the producer to the object (or idea) produced, (b) from the object (or idea) to the user. Of these two path sections I consider the second one important. If the "producer-object" section has a reduced importance, this means that it is not important to know *who made* a thing; the important thing is to know *for whom* it was made.

An "anonymous society," in which *anybody* knows how to make things which will be considered important, is necessarily an "egalitarian" society, based on nonpaternalist organization: such a society is anti-elitist.

3. Society with "weak communication"

When we investigated the idea of critical group, we saw that decisive factors were "valence" and "channel capacity." "Critical group" was thus a relatively small group with a very reduced amount of communication, as most communications could not reach persons situated far from the source (distance measured by the number of transmissions

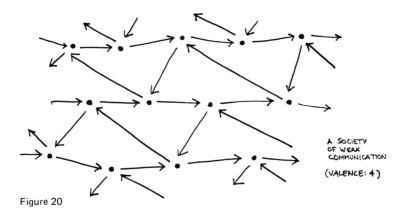

A SOCIETY
OF WEAK
COMMUNICATION
(VALENCE: 4)

Figure 20

necessary to convey influence).

We considered "critical group" as an "island" with a zone of non-communication surrounding it. But conditions for the critical group could be interpreted otherwise: in a communication network containing a number of persons and objects there can exist a critical group around each person (or object) in the society, considered as the "center" of this group. Such an interpretation is possible if the links composing the network are arranged in such a way that the number of links relating a particular person to the others does not exceed the number admitted by "valence."

This society, even though it contains a very large number of individuals, contains a relatively small number of links: if it is based on "weak communication."

A.4.4 INDIA AS A POSSIBLE ALTERNATIVE MODEL FOR WESTERN—TYPE SOCIETY

I find it rather interesting that the only place where I met an observable example of all three types of egalitarian society was India. Although noncompetitive society, anonymous society, and the society of weak communication exist *separately* in western-type countries, in India I observed all three together.

Indian society is composed of very small groups (smaller than the critical group). These groups are not linked very tightly by local communication because of technological inefficiency (to their benefit).

Indian artisans for many centuries have considered it undesirable to sign their work: it could be produced by anybody. What is considered important for a work (or product) is the way the future user will utilize it, and this way ("code") is strictly indicated.

Noncompetitive society does exist in India but in an incomplete form, since abundance, which would be necessary to its complete development, is lacking. But because of the poverty of the country, noncompetition characterizes the basic attitude of people: it is appreciated, contrary to the situation in our countries, where competition is admired as a positive, desirable feature.

It is not uninteresting to remark that industrial development in India (a development which is considerably more advanced than many people would think) is proceeding less by large industrial concentration than (always for technological reasons) by artisanal decentralization: artisans (workers) work at home for industrial organizations, and they often make up by inventiveness what they lack in tools.

I know that I cannot avoid being superficial and partial by the picture I have sketched. My intention here is less to discuss India's policy than to use what I observed to support the theoretic concepts stated before, knowing that the facts might develop in an unforeseeable way and that the reasoning behind them is complex, conditioned by a long history. Even so, I was fascinated to find that in this very rational country (the only one among developing countries where a military dictatorship has never existed), there exists a model from which we could, perhaps, learn something.

A.4.5 AN INDUSTRIAL "ECOSYSTEM"

The idea of relating the "critical group" of society to that of production (concepts linked by similar thresholds) led to the society of "weak communications," social and artisanal.

This idea could lead us even further toward a social and industrial "ecosystem," which could be successful provided that links are weak within the system. This system could be thus represented by a map in which "valence" and "channel capacity" would have very low numerical values.

I have been talking in the preceding sections about a "social ecosystem" (without using the expression). Let us look now very briefly at an industrial ecosystem.

It would be, to give it a concrete form, a "coexistence" of small-scale industrial organizations (smaller than the critical group). These organizations would function in such a way that waste produced by one would represent raw material for the other (similarly to the example of materials rejected by farmers becoming raw material for builders).

The waste of western industrial production could represent today, for example, a very important source of raw material for developing countries. Plastic bottles, food cans, cardboard wrappings, even newspapers are materials very intelligently used in India, or in other countries of an equal stage of development. Indians transform these materials into objects of beauty or of everyday use, objects which are often sought on the Western market!

An exchange of waste could be more important than the exchange of finished products going on today. Such an exchange could appeal to individual inventiveness within small groups (smaller than the critical group) and, on the other hand, it could prevent accumulation of industrial waste over the critical amount.

It seems to me quite probable that a social and industrial ecosystem having but weak internal communication could resolve most of our social, economic, and political problems.

A.5 LIMITED EFFECT OF TECHNOLOGICAL UTOPIAS

I have referred in this appendix mostly to social (or environmental) utopias. Why did I deliberately omit technological ones?

I will present here an example to show how small the direct impact of a technological utopia, even of a very advanced nature, could be. Let us suppose, for the sake of example only, that we can forecast implementation of some technological inventions (inventions which in reality are not yet out of laboratories). I choose here three inventions which could have a very large effect:
1. Advance control of weather
2. Large increase of staple food
3. Transport of energy with no conducting lines.

These three inventions could be realized in several ways:

1. By hardware ("things" used by man: satellite relay for weather control, "green revolution" for basic food, energy beams for energy transport)

2. By software (mutation of man himself: better weather resistance of the human body, better efficiency of human metabolism).

What would the earth's landscape become if these inventions could be implemented?

It would become (whether by hard or soft technology) a paradise: no buildings (as weather shelters would no longer be necessary), no towns, almost no factories. The only manmade objects visible on the landscape would be meeting places (where people would gather if their presence were necessary) and paths or roads leading to these areas.

Let us think. This utopia is not new: it existed in prehistoric times, when the only manmade objects were assembly places and paths leadinto to them.

The two pictures are identical. The most developed technology we can imagine leads us to prehistory.

If our species has changed since prehistory, this may be less the consequence of technology than of transformations of human social organizations.

This example is not intended as a proof, only to demonstrate the primordial importance of relations among individuals, which I consider to take precedence over technological inventions.

CONCLUSION

This short study led to very important results: the *possibilities of realization* of social or environmental utopias.

My first conclusion was that "society" and "environment" mean the same thing: a set of persons and objects around us. This equivalence of society and environment signifies, logically, that "structural laws" valid for the one are valid as well for the other. These laws are characterized by "threshold conditions," which means that both society and environment function differently above and below certain strictly definable dimensions: I called these thresholds the "critical group size" (for society) and "critical amount" (for objects in the environment).

Although "structural laws" are the same for both society and environment my moral attitude—conditioned by the fact that we are men and not objects—is a different one toward society than toward environment. As a matter of fact, I find admissible a "paternalist" attitude toward objects and I consider the same attitude inadmissible toward humans. I demand a nonpaternalist attitude toward men, which means that nobody has the right to make decisions for other people who might suffer from these decisions.

These two conclusions, one structural and the other moral, are not independent of each other: it is the structural law which determines what consequences (risks) can be expected from decisions we make, whether concerning society or environment.

For moral reasons, the most desirable society seems to be, in my opinion, the one I called "egalitarian." This type of society is considered utopian because it has not often been realized. Our new knowledge about critical groups shows the reasons for the apparent unrealizability of this type of society, which results from the fact that nearly every attempt to set up such a society passed limits imposed by the critical group.

We cannot improve the actual situation (social and environmental) by technological progress alone. Such progress, at best, only leads us back to some situation which existed before and which could be implemented as well without technological progress.

We cannot improve our society and our environment except under the condition that all improvements are decided on by all of us. This type of decision making is implied by the nonpaternalist scheme described earlier. The way to such improvement could be through a social and economic ecosystem with weak communication.

Critical group size, a fundamental condition of survival, is a characteristic of our species. Our future could depend on our answer to the question: can we get back to groups satisfying the criteria of critical group, or are we undergoing a "mutation" (in the biological sense) into another species characterized by a different critical group?

UNIVERSITY OF MICHIGAN

3 9015 04918 1228

38 25 MM 5389
BR4
01/09 02-013-01 Ohio

THE UNIVERSITY OF MICHIGAN

DATE DUE

EP 1 8 1989	
AY 1 0 1991	
JUL 0 5 1991	
APR 2 8 1992	
4 1993	
CT 4 1993	
AR 1 5 1994	
JAN 1 1 1995	
MAR 2 6 2002	
JAN 1 3 2009